Options Trading for Income: The Complete Guide

Master Cash-Secured Puts, Covered Calls, and Credit Spreads to Generate Income, Build Wealth, and Achieve Financial Freedom

CONTENTS

THE
ULTIMATE
WHEEL
STRATEGY
GUIDE
Three Steps To Generate Income and
Build Wealth With Options Even If You
Have No Trading Experience
SCHOLARLY MIND CREATIONS, LLC

Contents

Introduction

The Ultimate Wheel Strategy Guide

Of all the strategies I've taught clients to master, the most frequently requested, by far, is The Wheel. Its simplicity, versatility, and potential for consistent income make it a favorite among traders of all experience levels.

I've seen firsthand how The Wheel can transform portfolios when it's used correctly. I've also seen uneducated traders make costly mistakes, leaving money on the table and exposing themselves to unnecessary risks, which often result in avoidable losses. This book is designed to help you understand the reasons behind each step in this powerful strategy, so you can become a more effective trader.

Trading strategies come and go, with different strategies taking turns being touted as the "next big thing" only to fizzle out as market conditions change. But some strategies stand the test of time, proving their worth with consistent, real-world results. The Wheel is one such.

What makes The Wheel so compelling is its simplicity. To effectively utilize The Wheel, you don't need to predict the next market crash or boom or decipher complex charts. The strength of The Wheel is that it's a methodical, repeatable process that leverages the power of options to both generate income and acquire quality stocks at prices you choose. It's a strategy for the patient, the disciplined, and those who understand that consistent success over time will outperform wild risks in the long run.

The Wheel isn't flashy, but it works. It works well. And it's repeatable. Whether you're new to options or you've been trading for years, The Wheel offers a simple way to trade with confidence and improve your returns without being glued to the your computer screen all day.

My goal is to make The Wheel strategy accessible to everyone, whether you're new to trading or an experienced trader, this book will break down the concepts, eliminate confusion, and help you build confidence in using this powerful strategy to generate income and grow your wealth.

Why The Wheel Strategy?

If you've spent any time exploring trading strategies, you've likely encountered a wide range of strategies: day trading, swing trading, long-term investing, credit spreads, debit spreads, butterflies, strangles, condors, calendars, and everything in between. Many of these methods require significant time, energy, and often a bit of luck to succeed. The Wheel, on the other hand, is different. It's designed to generate long-term growth and short-term income by using options in a systematic way.

At its core, The Wheel has three key steps:

1. **Selling Cash-Secured Puts**: You earn income by selling options that obligate you to buy a stock you like at a price you choose, but only if the stock drops to that level.
2. **Selling Covered Calls**: Once you own the stock, you benefit from appreciation and enhance your returns by selling options that oblige you to sell your shares at a price you choose.
3. **Repeat**.

This cycle: sell puts, acquire stock, sell calls, sell stock, repeats like a wheel in motion, hence the name.

When trading The Wheel, you have the ability to easily adjust the parameters to match the trade with your goals, risk tolerance, and market outlook. Do you want to prioritize income? Great, adjust your strike prices and expirations accordingly. Looking to acquire shares of a stock you believe in long-term? Great, adjust your strike prices and expiration dates to utilize The Wheel as a tool to buy in at a discount while generating income along the way.

Why Now Is the Right Time for The Wheel

The financial markets are ever-changing, and strategies that work in one climate often fail in another. What makes The Wheel unique is its ability to work in multiple market conditions and compound growth the over time.

The Wheel is a practical and reliable strategy that eliminates the guesswork and "gambling" often associated with trading options, while providing better returns than stock trading alone. For investors seeking stability and predictable returns amidst uncertainty, this strategy will help you achieve the success you're looking for.

Dispelling Common Misconceptions

Many people shy away from options trading because they are afraid it's too complicated or risky. While it's true that options can be complex, and they can be used for risky speculative trades, The Wheel is neither. This strategy focuses on prudent, calculated moves, and defined risks. Success with The Wheel simply requires you to understand your obligations as an options seller and to use those obligations to your advantage.

Another misconception is that trading options requires extensive market knowledge or constant monitoring. While some awareness of market conditions is helpful, The Wheel doesn't demand that you stare at screens all day. In fact, many Wheel traders set up their trades, go about their lives, and only check back periodically. Success with The Wheel isn't a result of trading all day, it's a result of having a plan and sticking to it.

A Strategy That Works in Real Life

A few years ago, one of my clients, let's call him Greg, approached me with a problem that many investors face. Greg was primarily a long-term investor who had grown frustrated with the constant ups and downs of the stock market. He wasn't just annoyed by the volatility; he felt stuck. While his portfolio included some solid, dividend-paying stocks, a large portion of his capital was sitting idle in cash, earning next to nothing. Greg wanted more than just the passive trickle of dividend income, he wanted his money to work harder for him.

When Greg first shared his concerns, I could tell he wasn't looking for a quick-fix solution or a high-risk gamble. He wanted something practical, reliable, and aligned with his belief in building wealth over time. That's when I introduced him to The Wheel strategy.

The concept was new to Greg, but he was intrigued by its simplicity and potential. We started with small steps. I explained how he could use the stocks he already owned to generate income by selling covered calls, essentially renting out his shares to earn premiums. For the cash sitting in his portfolio, I showed him how to sell cash-secured puts on stocks he believed in—effectively earning income while positioning himself to buy those stocks at a discount if the opportunity arose.

At first, Greg was cautious, dipping his toes into the strategy with a few trades. But as he began to see results, his confidence grew. Within just a few months, he was generating consistent income from his existing stocks while putting his idle cash to productive use. Even better, he found himself building a portfolio of companies he genuinely believed in, aligning his long-term investment goals with the short-term benefits of The Wheel.

Greg's success wasn't due to insider knowledge or sheer luck. It came down to following the core principles you'll learn in this book: discipline, patience, and a focus on manageable trades. He stuck to the process, avoided chasing the market, and made decisions based on sound strategy rather than emotion.

His story is proof that The Wheel strategy isn't just for experienced traders or financial experts. It's a tool that can work for anyone who is willing to learn, adapt, and apply its principles. Whether you're like Greg, tired of market fluctuations and seeking a more reliable way to grow your wealth, or simply curious about maximizing your portfolio's potential, this book will show you how The Wheel can transform your approach to investing.

Who Is This Book For?

This book is for anyone who wants to take control of their financial future. Whether you're:

- **A beginner** looking for a straightforward, easy-to-follow strategy to enter the world of options trading without feeling overwhelmed,
- **An experienced trader** searching for a consistent and reliable way to generate income in both stable and volatile markets,

- **Or a long-term investor** frustrated with the limitations of the traditional "buy low, sell high" approach and eager to explore a strategy that works in a variety of market conditions,

The Wheel strategy has something to offer you. It doesn't require you to predict the next big market trend or spend hours glued to your screen. Instead, it rewards discipline, patience, and consistency. This makes it an ideal approach for anyone who wants to make their money work harder, whether you're managing a retirement portfolio, saving for a specific goal, or simply looking to build wealth over time.

What You'll Learn

In this book, we'll break down The Wheel strategy into clear, actionable steps that anyone can follow. You don't need a background in finance or years of trading experience to succeed. By the time you finish, you'll have the tools and knowledge to start using The Wheel with confidence.

Here's what we'll cover:

- **How to identify the best stocks for The Wheel.** Not all stocks are created equal, and knowing which ones to target is the foundation of this strategy.

- **How to select strike prices and expiration dates.** Learn how to structure your trades to align with your financial goals, risk tolerance, and market outlook.

- **The pros and cons of in-the-money, at-the-money, and out-of-the-money options.** Discover how these choices affect your trades and when to adjust your approach for maximum profitability.

- **How to navigate different market scenarios.** Whether prices are falling, stagnating, or surging, you'll learn strategies to keep earning income while managing your risks.

- **Advanced techniques for optimizing your trades.** Dive deeper into adjustments, rolling positions, and other methods to enhance your results and mitigate potential losses.
- **How to create a long-term plan.** Learn how to integrate The Wheel into your overall portfolio strategy, so you can grow your wealth steadily over time.

How to Use This Book Effectively

This book is designed to be both a comprehensive guide and a practical toolkit. If you're new to options, I recommend starting with Options 101. This chapter will introduce you to the basics of options trading and help you become familiar with the terminology used throughout the rest of this book.

For experienced traders, feel free to skip ahead to the Mechanics of the Wheel Strategy chapter. This chapter will help you become familiar with the specifics of The Wheel strategy and build a solid foundation which we will build on for the rest of the book.

Getting Started

As you embark on this journey, it's important to understand that every trader's path is unique. While this book is packed with examples, techniques, and strategies to guide you, they are not one-size-fits-all solutions. Instead, think of them as building blocks, a foundation upon which you can construct your own approach. Your financial goals, risk tolerance, and personal circumstances will play a crucial role in shaping how you apply what you learn here.

It's also worth remembering that no strategy, including The Wheel, comes with guaranteed success. Past performance, no matter how impressive, is not a promise of future results. Markets are dynamic and unpredictable, which is why adaptability and a willingness to learn are as important as the strategy itself.

That said, the beauty of The Wheel lies in its simplicity and versatility. Whether you're looking to generate consistent income, grow your wealth over time, or simply expand your trading skills, this strategy can be tailored to meet your needs. The journey you're about to take is as much about personal growth as it is about financial success.

So, as you dive in, take the time to practice, refine your technique, and make adjustments that keep your trades aligned with your unique goals. The tools and knowledge you gain from this book are yours to shape, refine, and use as you step into the exciting world of options trading. Your first spin begins now, let's get started!

CHAPTER 1

OPTIONS 101

THE BASICS

OPTIONS TRADING CAN SEEM intimidating at first, but with a solid understanding of the fundamentals, anyone can learn to navigate this dynamic and lucrative market. In this chapter, we'll break down the essential concepts of options trading, provide beginner-friendly scenarios, and offer a glossary of key terms to help you build a strong foundation.

Understanding the basics of calls and puts is essential for mastering more advanced strategies like The Wheel. Selling cash-secured puts and covered calls (the core of The Wheel strategy) both rely on these foundational principles.

By starting here, you'll develop the knowledge needed to confidently navigate options trading and begin exploring how to generate consistent income through strategic use of options.

In the next chapter, we'll dive deeper into how The Wheel works, breaking down its components step by step and showing you how to put these fundamentals into action.

Glossary of Key Terms

Understanding the basic terminology of options trading is crucial to following the concepts and strategies outlined in this book. Below is a glossary of the most common terms you'll encounter. While some will be explained in greater detail later, this section provides enough context to grasp the basics.

- **Underlying Asset:** The stock, ETF, index, or other financial instrument on which an option is based. For example, if you're trading an option on Apple (AAPL), the stock itself is the underlying asset.
- **Call Options:** These allow the buyer to purchase the underlying asset at the strike price if they choose to do so. The seller of the call option agrees to sell the asset at the strike price if the buyer exercises their right.
- **Put Options:** These allow the buyer to sell the underlying asset at the strike price if they choose to do so. The seller of the put option agrees to buy the asset at the strike price if the buyer exercises their right.
- **Strike Price:** The specified price at which the buyer of an option can buy (in the case of a call) or sell (in the case of a put) the underlying asset.

- **Expiration Date**: Options are time-sensitive contracts, so this date marks the end of their life cycle. After expiration, the option ceases to exist.
- **Premium**: The price the buyer pays to the seller for the option contract. This amount compensates the seller for taking on the risks and obligations associated with the option contract.
- **Exercise**: The act of the option buyer using their right to buy (call) or sell (put) the underlying asset at the strike price.
- **Assignment**: This occurs when the seller of an option is notified that the buyer has exercised their option. The seller must fulfill their obligation, either selling (in the case of a call) or buying (in the case of a put) the underlying asset at the strike price.
- **In-the-Money (ITM)**: When an option's strike price makes it profitable to exercise. For calls, this happens when the stock price is above the strike price. For puts, this happens when the stock price is below the strike price.
- **At-the-Money (ATM):** When the option's strike price is roughly equal to the stock's current price, making it balanced between potential profit and loss.
- **Out-of-the-Money (OTM)**: When an option's strike price makes it unprofitable to exercise. For calls, this happens when the stock price is below the strike price. For puts, this happens when the stock price is above the strike price.
- **Time Decay (Theta)**: The gradual reduction in an option's price as it gets closer to its expiration date. This happens because there is less time for the stock price to move in a way that makes the option more valuable. Time decay accelerates as expiration approaches, especially for options that are not profitable to exercise.

The History of Options

The concept of options trading dates back centuries. In ancient Greece, philosopher Thales used an early form of options to speculate on olive press usage, securing contracts for presses at a set price before a harvest. He profited when demand for presses surged during a bountiful harvest season.

Modern options trading, however, began in 1973 with the establishment of the Chicago Board Options Exchange (CBOE). This standardized options contracts and introduced pricing models like the Black-Scholes formula, revolutionizing the market.

In recent years, technological advancements have played a pivotal role in democratizing options trading. Online brokerage platforms have made it easier than ever for retail investors to access options markets, providing tools for analysis, real-time data, and educational resources. As a result, the number of retail traders using options has surged, making it one of the most popular tools for income generation and risk management today.

What Are Options?

Modern options are financial contracts between two people. Each contract gives the buyer the right, but not the obligation, to buy or sell an underlying asset at a specified price (the strike price) before the specified expiration date. The seller of the option, is paid up-front in exchange for taking on an obligation to fulfill the contract if the buyer chooses to exercise their right.

Options are derivatives, meaning that they derive their value from an underlying asset. The underlying asset can be a stock, an index, or even commodities like oil or gold. In this book, we'll focus on US stock options, which are the most common type for retail traders.

Options are traded in contracts, with each contract representing control of 100 shares of the underlying asset. For example, if you buy one call option for a stock, it gives you the right to buy 100 shares of that stock at the strike price.

When you buy an option, you pay a premium to the seller. This premium is determined by factors such as:

- The stock's current price relative to the strike price.
- The time remaining until expiration.
- The stock's expected future volatility.

How Options Are Priced

Options pricing is more easily explained if we break it into two primary components: **Intrinsic Value** and **Extrinsic Value**.

Intrinsic Value

Intrinsic Value refers to the real, tangible value an option has if exercised immediately. It is calculated by taking the difference between the current stock price and the option's strike price. Intrinsic value is always a positive number or zero (it cannot be negative). Here's how it works for both call and put options:

Call Options:

For a call option, intrinsic value exists when the stock price is higher than the option's strike price. This is because the buyer has the right to purchase shares at the lower strike price and could sell them at the higher market price, capturing the difference as profit.

- **Example:** If a call option has a strike price of $50 and the stock is trading at $60, the intrinsic value of the option is $10 ($60 - $50).

- If the stock price is below the strike price (e.g., stock at $40 with a $50 strike price), the call option has no intrinsic value because exercising it would require buying shares for more than they're worth on the open market. In this case, the intrinsic value is $0.

Put Options:

For a put option, intrinsic value exists when the stock price is lower than the option's strike price. This is because the buyer has the right to sell shares at the higher strike price while the market price is lower, capturing the difference as profit.

- **Example:** If a put option has a strike price of $50 and the stock is trading at $40, the intrinsic value is $10 ($50 - $40).
- If the stock price is above the strike price (e.g., stock at $60 with a $50 strike price), the put option has no intrinsic value. This is because selling shares at the lower strike price when they could be sold for more in the open market would result in a loss. In this case, the intrinsic value is $0.

Intrinsic value only applies to **in-the-money options** (calls where the stock price is above the strike price, and puts where the stock price is below the strike price).

Out-of-the-money options (calls where the stock price is below the strike price and puts where the stock price is above the strike price) have no intrinsic value, though they may still have value due to their time value or potential future price movements until they expire.

Extrinsic Value

Extrinsic Value is the portion of an option's price that is not tied to its intrinsic value. It is also known as "time value" or "premium value" and reflects the market's expectations for how the stock price might move before the option expires. Both call and put options will have extrinsic value until they expire, regardless of whether they are in-the-money, at-the-money, or out-of-the-money.

Call Options:

For call options, extrinsic value arises from the potential that the stock price will rise above the strike price before expiration. It depends on factors like time remaining until expiration, volatility, and interest rates.

- **Example:** If a call option has a strike price of $50 and the stock is trading at $60, the option's intrinsic value is $10. If the total premium (price) of the option is $15, the extrinsic value is $5 ($15 - $10).
- If the stock price is at $40 (below the strike price), the call option has no intrinsic value. However, the premium might still be $2 due to extrinsic value, which reflects the market's belief that the stock could rise above the strike price before expiration.

Put Options:

For put options, extrinsic value reflects the potential for the stock price to fall below the strike price before the option expires. Like calls, extrinsic value for puts is influenced by time remaining, volatility, and market conditions.

- **Example:** If a put option has a strike price of $50 and the stock is trading at $40, the option's intrinsic value is $10. If the total premium is $13, the extrinsic value is $3 ($13 - $10).
- If the stock price is at $60 (above the strike price), the put option has no intrinsic value. However, if it still had a premium of $2 that would be entirely extrinsic value, reflecting the chance that the stock price could fall below the strike price before expiration.

Factors That Impact Extrinsic Value:

1. **Time to Expiration:** Options with more time left until expiration have higher extrinsic value because there's a greater chance for the stock price to move favorably.
2. **Volatility:** Higher stock volatility increases extrinsic value since the stock price is more likely to make significant moves. The higher premium compensates sellers for taking on higher risk positions.
3. **Interest Rates:** For call options, higher interest rates can slightly increase extrinsic value because it costs less to buy the option than to hold cash for a stock purchase.
4. **Market Sentiment:** Demand for certain options can raise their extrinsic value, as more traders speculate on potential stock movements.

Key Points to Remember:

- Extrinsic value is present in all options before expiration, regardless of whether they are in-the-money, at-the-money, or out-of-the-money.
- At-the-money options (where the stock price equals the strike price) tend to have the highest extrinsic value because there's maximum uncertainty about which way the stock will move.
- As expiration approaches, extrinsic value decreases. By expiration, the extrinsic value of all options becomes $0, leaving only intrinsic value for in-the-money options.

Why Understanding Intrinsic and Extrinsic Value Matters for Option Sellers

When selling options, you are primarily selling extrinsic value. Understanding the difference between intrinsic and extrinsic value is critical to managing risk and maximizing profitability. As expiration approaches, extrinsic value diminishes. If the option expires out-of-the-money, the seller keeps the entire premium as profit.

How to Read an Option Chain

An option chain is a table that displays all available option contracts for a specific stock, organized by expiration date and strike price. It provides essential information that traders use to evaluate and select trades. Most brokerages allow you to customize the option chain to display the data you feel is most relevant. This flexibility lets you tailor the chain to suit your strategy and focus on the metrics that matter most to you. Here's how to interpret and customize the key components:

1. Strike Prices

Strike prices are listed in the center column of the chain and are displayed from lowest to highest, with prices increasing the further you scroll down. These represent the prices at which the stock can be bought (calls) or sold (puts) if the option is exercised. Strike prices closer to the stock's current price are typically more actively traded and sensitive to price movements. Strikes further away from the current price reflect more speculative options, often with lower probability but potentially higher returns.

2. Bid and Ask Prices

The bid price is the highest amount a buyer is willing to pay for the option, while the ask price is the lowest amount a seller is willing to accept. The difference between these prices, known as the bid-ask spread, is a good indicator of the liquidity of the option. Narrower spreads mean better liquidity, making it easier to enter and exit positions at favorable prices. Displaying the bid and ask prices will help you to estimate liquidity as well as help you determine the cost to enter or exit a trade.

3. Implied Volatility (IV)

Implied Volatility reflects the market's expectations for the stock's future price swings. Higher IV typically leads to more expensive option premiums, as the perceived risk increases. Many traders use IV to identify opportunities: high IV may signal overpriced options, ideal for selling strategies, while low IV may indicate undervalued options, suitable for buying strategies. Displaying IV on your chain helps you assess potential trade value.

4. Open Interest

Open Interest shows the total number of contracts for an option that are currently open (not yet exercised or closed). Options with high open interest are usually easier to trade because they have better liquidity. Including open interest in your chain view helps you avoid options with low trading activity, which can be harder to buy or sell without incurring significant costs.

5. Volume

Option chains often include volume, which measures the number of contracts traded during the current trading session. High volume indicates strong market interest in an option and often correlates with tighter bid-ask spreads. Tracking volume can help you identify where the market is most active, providing insights into potential price movements.

6. Greeks

Many brokerages allow you to display the option Greeks: Delta, Gamma, Theta, Vega, and Rho, which measure different aspects of an option's risk and reward. Each Greek provides unique insights into how the option's price reacts to changes in the stock price, time, or volatility. A more detailed explanation of each Greek is provided below. Including these metrics in your chain view helps you make more informed decisions based on your specific trading goals.

Customizing the option chain to include the data most relevant to your trading style can save time and improve decision-making.

The Greeks: Simplified

Understanding the Greeks is essential for any options trader. These are metrics that help you evaluate the behavior of an option under different conditions:

- **Delta**: Measures how much the price of an option will change for every $1 change in the underlying stock's price. For example, a Delta of 0.5 means the option's price will increase by $0.50 per share, or $50 for a standard contract (100 shares), for every $1 rise in the stock price.
- **Theta**: Represents the impact of time decay. As an option approaches its expiration date, its value decreases due to the diminishing time left to make a profit.
- **Vega**: Indicates how much an option's price changes with a 1% change in implied volatility. Higher volatility means higher premiums, as there's a greater likelihood of the stock price moving significantly.
- **Rho:** Indicates how much an option's price will change with each percentage change in the risk-free interest rate. For most retail traders this value can be ignored as the changes are minimal when compared to the other Greeks.

Understanding these factors helps traders predict how their options will perform under various scenarios, and helps you to make more informed decisions.

The Difference Between Historical and Implied Volatility

Volatility plays a significant role in options pricing and comes in two primary forms, each providing different insights for traders. Understanding the difference between historical volatility and implied volatility (IV) is essential for evaluating option strategies and managing risk.

1. **Historical Volatility (HV)**: Historical volatility measures how much a stock's price has fluctuated over a specific period in the past. It is calculated using actual price movements, often expressed as an annualized percentage. HV provides a sense of how stable or volatile a stock has been historically, helping traders understand its past behavior. Historical volatility serves as a benchmark for comparing a stock's current activity to its past trends. If the current price movement significantly deviates from its historical volatility, it might indicate an unusual market event or changing conditions. However, HV only reflects past price behavior and cannot predict future price movements. It is backward-looking and does not account for potential upcoming events that could increase or decrease volatility.

2. **Implied Volatility (IV)**: Implied volatility reflects the market's expectations for a stock's future price fluctuations. It is forward-looking and derived from the current prices of options. IV indicates how much price movement the market anticipates, often spiking before major events like earnings announcements, product launches, or economic reports. IV directly impacts option premiums. Higher IV means higher premiums because the market expects significant price movements, increasing the likelihood of options expiring in-the-money. Conversely, lower IV often leads to cheaper options, as less price fluctuation is anticipated. Unlike HV, which is static once calculated, IV constantly

changes based on market sentiment, demand for options, and upcoming events.

For options traders, implied volatility is particularly critical because it shapes option pricing and potential profitability. Here's why understanding the difference between HV and IV is important:

- **Evaluating Option Pricing:** Comparing HV and IV can help identify whether options are overpriced or underpriced. For example, if IV is significantly higher than HV, the market might be overestimating future volatility, creating opportunities for option sellers.
- **Strategy Selection:** High IV environments are ideal for selling strategies, such as covered calls or credit spreads, where traders benefit from inflated premiums. Low IV environments, on the other hand, are often better for buying strategies, like long calls or puts, where cheaper premiums reduce upfront costs.
- **Risk Management:** Knowing how IV behaves can help traders anticipate potential price swings around key events and adjust their positions accordingly to mitigate risk.

The Risk and Reward of Options

Visualizing Profits and Risks of Options

Options provide distinct risk and reward profiles, differing significantly from the straightforward risks and rewards of buying or selling stocks. Understanding these dynamics is essential for managing your trades effectively and aligning your strategy with your risk tolerance.

Risk

- **For Buyers:** The maximum risk for option buyers is limited to the premium paid for the contract. This makes buying options a defined-risk strategy. Whether the stock moves against the buyer or remains stagnant, the loss cannot exceed the initial cost of the option. This feature makes options appealing to traders looking for high leverage with controlled downside risk.
    - **Example:** If you buy a call option for $2.50 per share (or $250 total for one contract), and the stock price stays below the strike price until expiration, your total loss is $250, no matter how low the stock price falls.
- **For Sellers:** The main risk for sellers comes from being required to fulfill their obligation under the option contract:
    - **Selling Calls:** When selling a call, the seller is obligated to sell the underlying stock at the strike price if the buyer exercises the option. If the stock price rises significantly above the strike price, the seller could face large losses, especially if they don't already own the shares (naked call). For example, if the stock price soars far above the strike price, the seller must purchase shares at the higher market price and sell them at the lower strike price.
    - **Selling Puts:** When selling a put, the seller is obligated to buy the underlying stock at the strike price if the buyer exercises the option. If the stock price falls far below the strike price, the seller could be forced to buy shares at a much higher price than their current market value. For example, if the stock drops to zero, the seller must still buy the shares at the agreed strike price, even though the stock is worthless.

Reward

- **For Buyers:**

- **Calls:** Buyers of call options can profit significantly if the stock price rises well above the strike price. The potential reward is unlimited because stock prices have no upper limit.
- **Puts:** Buyers of put options can profit if the stock price falls well below the strike price, with the maximum reward achieved when the stock price drops to zero.

- **For Sellers:** The reward for sellers is limited to the premium they receive for selling the option. This is the maximum profit the seller can make, regardless of how favorable the stock price movement is.

The contrasting risk and reward profiles between buyers and sellers define how options are used in trading strategies. Buyers aim for large potential profits with limited risk, making options attractive for speculative trades or hedging. Sellers, on the other hand, seek consistent income by collecting premiums, accepting defined or unlimited risk depending on the strategy, in exchange for a higher probability of success.

Using Diagrams to Visualize Options Risks and Rewards

To help solidify these concepts, a diagram of a basic profit and loss graph (P&L graph) for call and put options can be highly effective. These diagrams reveal the trends each position will benefit from, and which trends will result in a loss.

Call Options:

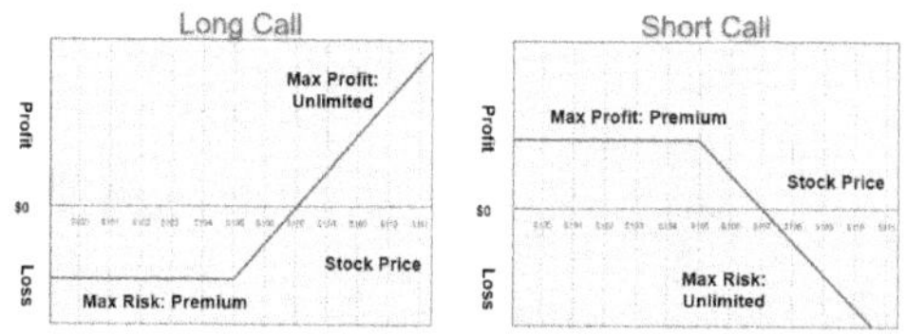

- The x-axis represents the stock price.

- The y-axis represents the profit or loss.

Long Call: The P&L graph for a long call slopes upward to the right, showing that the option becomes more valuable as the stock price rises. This reflects the potential profit a long call generates when the stock moves in a bullish direction. A long call gives the buyer the right to purchase shares at a specific strike price. The higher the stock price climbs above the strike price, the more valuable the option becomes.

On the loss side of the graph, a flat line extends to the left of the strike price. This indicates that the maximum loss is capped at the premium paid for the option. Even if the stock price stays low or falls further, the most you can lose is what you initially invested. On the profit side, there is no limit because a stock price can, in theory, rise indefinitely, allowing for unlimited potential gains.

Short Call: The P&L graph for a short call slopes downward to the right, representing the increasing losses a seller faces as the stock price rises. A short call obligates the seller to sell shares at the strike price. If the stock price exceeds the strike price, the seller could be forced to buy shares at a higher market price and sell them at a loss. If the seller already owns the shares, they won't incur a financial loss but will miss out on any gains beyond the strike price.

The graph also shows a flat line on the profit side, extending to the left of the strike price. This reflects the maximum profit for a short call, which is limited to the premium received when the option was sold. As long as the stock price remains below the strike price, the seller keeps the full premium.

Put Options:

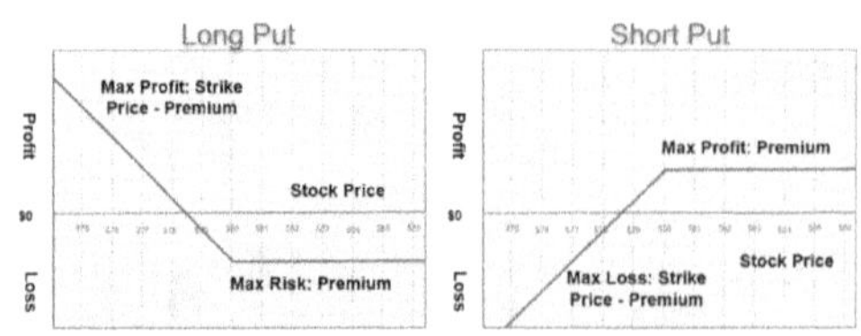

- The x-axis represents the stock price.
- The y-axis represents the profit or loss.

Long Put: The P&L graph for a long put slopes upward to the left, showing that the option becomes more valuable as the stock price falls. A long put profits when the underlying stock moves bearishly. This is because the contract gives the buyer the right to sell shares at the strike price. The lower the stock price drops below the strike price, the more valuable the option becomes, as the buyer could sell shares for more than they're worth on the market.

On the loss side, the graph shows a flat line extending to the right of the strike price. This indicates that the maximum loss is limited to the premium paid for the option. Even if the stock price rises significantly, the most you can lose is your initial investment. The potential gain for a long put is substantial, as the lower a stock price goes, the more valuable the option becomes, though the maximum profit occurs when the stock price falls to zero.

Short Put: The P&L graph for a short put slopes downward to the left, reflecting increasing losses as the stock price drops. A short put obligates the seller to buy shares at the strike price if the stock falls below that level. If this happens, the seller may have to purchase shares for more than their current market value, resulting in a loss. The lower the stock price falls, the greater the potential loss for the seller.

The graph also shows a flat line on the profit side, extending to the right of the strike price. This represents the maximum profit, which is limited to the premium received for selling the put. The seller keeps the full premium as long as the stock price remains above the strike price. However, if the stock price drops below the strike price, the seller starts incurring losses.

Practical Tips for Beginners

Starting with options can feel overwhelming, with new traders not knowing where to start. So, here are some practical tips to set yourself up for success right from the beginning:

1. **Choose the Right Brokerage Platform**: Look for a platform that provides comprehensive tools for options trading. Features to prioritize include real-time data, intuitive options chains, risk management tools, and educational resources. Low commission rates and a user-friendly interface can also make your trading experience smoother.

2. **Start Small**: When you're new to options, it's wise to trade just one contract at a time until you become more proficient. This helps you manage risk while you're learning the ropes. Over time, as your confidence and knowledge grows, you can scale up your trading activity.

3. **Focus on Liquidity**: Begin by trading options on highly liquid stocks. This makes it easier to enter and exit trades and reduces the likelihood that you will be "stuck" in a trade.

4. **Set Realistic Expectations**: Options trading isn't a quick path to wealth, it's a skill that requires patience, discipline, and a clear understanding of risk. Start with achievable goals, allowing you to celebrate small wins along the way as you learn. These early successes build confidence and motivation while you sharpen your skills. As your knowledge and experience grows, you can safely scale up and aim for larger returns.

Common Misconceptions and Mistakes

Options trading can be a powerful tool, but it's also filled with pitfalls that can trip up beginners. By understanding these common misconceptions and mistakes, you can avoid costly errors and build a more solid foundation for success. Here are some of the most frequent issues to watch out for:

1. Ignoring Time Decay: Many new traders underestimate the impact of time decay on options. As expiration approaches, the time value of an option decreases, often at an accelerating pace. This means that even if the stock moves in the desired direction, the option may lose value if it doesn't move far enough or fast enough to offset the value lost due to time decay.

- **The Misconception:** Beginners often think that simply being correct about the stock's direction will lead to profits, without accounting for how much and how quickly the stock needs to move.
- **The Fix:** Be mindful of how much time is left until expiration and consider purchasing options with more time (longer expiration dates) to reduce the impact of time decay.

2. Choosing Inappropriate Strike Prices: Selecting the right strike price is crucial for successful options trading. Beginners often gravitate toward out-of-the-money options because they are cheaper, but these options also have a lower probability of becoming profitable.

- **The Misconception:** Thinking that cheaper options are always better. While lower premiums are attractive to buyers, they often reflect the reduced likelihood of the option becoming profitable.
- **The Fix:** Balance affordability with probability. Consider at-the-money or slightly in-the-money options if you're looking for a better chance of profitability, even if the premiums are higher.

3. Over-Leveraging: The leverage that options provide can amplify both gains and losses. Beginners may be tempted to invest large portions of their capital in options, chasing big wins without fully appreciating the risks. This can lead to significant losses if the trade doesn't go as planned.

- **The Misconception:** Believing that options are a shortcut to quick wealth, leading to overconfidence and excessive risk-taking.

- **The Fix:** Start with small, manageable positions. Use only a portion of your capital for each trade, and diversify your portfolio to spread risk.

4. Misunderstanding Implied Volatility: Many beginners overlook the role of implied volatility (IV) in options pricing. High IV can inflate premiums, making options more expensive, while low IV can lead to undervalued options. Failing to account for IV can result in overpaying for options or misjudging their true value.

- **The Misconception:** Assuming that an option's price is solely based on the underlying stock's performance, without considering market expectations.

- **The Fix:** Learn to analyze IV and compare it to historical volatility to gauge whether options are overpriced or underpriced.

5. Neglecting a Trading Plan: Without a clear plan, beginners may make impulsive decisions, such as holding onto losing trades for too long or selling winners too early. This lack of discipline can lead to inconsistent results.

- **The Misconception:** Thinking you can "wing it" and still achieve consistent profits.

- **The Fix:** Create a trading plan that includes entry and exit strategies, risk management rules, and clear goals. Stick to your plan to avoid emotional decision-making.

By understanding and avoiding these common pitfalls, you can set yourself up for success. Remember, every mistake is an opportunity to learn, and taking the time to master the basics will pay off in the long run. Whether it's being mindful of time decay, choosing appropriate strike prices, or managing your leverage, a disciplined approach will help you navigate the complexities of options trading with greater confidence.

Chapter 2

The Mechanics of The Wheel

Simplifying the Most Popular Income Strategy in Options

The Wheel strategy offers a unique advantage to traditional stock investing: the ability to generate income while building wealth. Unlike simply buying and holding stocks, where your profits depend solely on price appreciation, The Wheel leverages the power of options to create multiple streams of income and opportunities for higher profits. This strategy allows you to take control of your investments and maximize returns with less reliance on market timing or luck.

The Wheel strategy revolves around three distinct steps:

Step 1: Sell Cash-Secured Puts:

Start by selling put options on a stock you'd like to own. By selling these options, you are agreeing to purchase the stock at a specific price, which you select in advance. To ensure you can fulfill this obligation, you keep enough cash in your account to cover the purchase, hence the term "cash-secured." In exchange for taking on this obligation, you get paid a “premium.” This premium is yours to keep regardless of the outcome of the trade.

- If the stock price stays above the agreed price, you won’t need to buy the shares, the option will simply expire worthless and you will keep the premium. When this happens, you restart the process and sell another cash-secured put to generate more income.

- If the stock price falls below the price where you agreed to buy it, you purchase the shares at the agreed-upon price, and then move on to Step 2 of The Wheel.

Step 2: Sell Covered Calls:

Once you own the stock (whether through put assignment or because you already had the shares), you sell call options against the shares. By selling calls you are agreeing to sell your shares for a specific price, which you select in advance. In exchange for taking on this obligation, you get paid a “premium.” This premium is yours to keep regardless of the outcome of the trade.

- If the stock price stays below the agreed upon price, you keep your shares and the premium you received for selling the options. You can then sell another covered call to bring in additional income, and continue the cycle.

- If the stock price rises above the price where you agreed to sell your shares, you will keep the premium you received from selling the calls as well as the appreciation on the shares up to the price where the shares are "called away." This places an upper limit on your maximum profit, but it's a limit you get to decide

Step 3: Repeat:

Once your shares are sold, you return to Step 1 and start the process again by selling more cash-secured puts. This cycle of selling puts, acquiring shares, selling calls, selling shares, creates a continuous loop of income generation, making The Wheel both simple and highly effective.

- The Wheel strategy is a disciplined framework for maximizing the value of your portfolio. By repeating this process, you can systematically accumulate quality stocks at discounted prices, sell them for a profit, and reinvest the proceeds to keep the cycle going. Unlike traditional investing, where returns depend largely on market movements, The Wheel allows you to profit in various market conditions while maintaining control over your investments.

In this chapter, we'll break down each step of The Wheel in detail. You'll learn how to identify the best stocks for this strategy, select optimal strike prices and expiration dates, and manage risks to minimize potential losses. Through examples and actionable insights, you'll gain a clear understanding of how The Wheel works and how to apply it effectively in your own portfolio. By the end, you'll have the tools to turn The Wheel into a reliable and repeatable strategy for building wealth and generating income.

Finding the Right Stocks for The Wheel Strategy

Selecting the right stocks is a cornerstone of success with The Wheel strategy. While the strategy itself is straightforward, your results will largely depend on the quality of the equities you choose to trade. A thoughtful approach to stock selection not only increases your chances of profitability but also helps you manage risk more effectively.

Start with What You Know

One of the best ways to begin your search is by focusing on industries and sectors you are already familiar with. If you have a background in technology, healthcare, retail, or any other field, your understanding of that industry can give you a distinct advantage. Familiarity allows you to evaluate companies with greater confidence and spot trends that may not be immediately obvious to the general public.

For instance, during the 1990s, the technology sector boomed as the internet revolution took off, leading to significant growth for companies like Microsoft and Cisco. Similarly, in the 2000s, energy companies thrived as rising oil prices drew investor attention to the sector. More recently, industries like renewable energy and electric vehicles have captured investor interest, with stocks like Tesla dominating headlines. By focusing on industries you understand, you position yourself to capitalize on such trends more effectively.

Look for Resilient and Stable Stocks

While industry familiarity is an excellent starting point, the next step is to identify individual stocks that align with The Wheel strategy's goals. Ideal candidates often share these characteristics:

Mid- to Large-Cap Stocks

Focus on companies with substantial market capitalizations. These stocks tend to have greater liquidity, making it easier to enter and exit positions. Additionally, larger companies are often more stable and less prone to extreme price swings, which suits the cyclical nature of The Wheel.

Consistent Volatility

Stocks with moderate and predictable price fluctuations are often ideal. Too little volatility means the premiums from selling options will be low, reducing your potential income. Excessive volatility, on the other hand, can lead to significant losses if the stock moves sharply against you. Look for stocks with a healthy balance, enough movement to generate worthwhile premiums without excessive risk.

Strong Fundamentals

Pay attention to a company's financial health. Stocks with solid earnings growth, manageable debt levels, and a competitive position in their industry make better long-term candidates for ownership. Tools like price-to-earnings (P/E) ratios, return on equity (ROE), and dividend history can provide valuable insights into a company's quality.

Fairly Priced or Undervalued Stocks

Stocks that are fairly priced or undervalued relative to their intrinsic worth are often excellent candidates. Not only do they present a lower risk of sharp declines, but they also offer potential upside if the market corrects its valuation over time.

Active Options Markets

Ensure the stocks you select have active options markets with tight bid-ask spreads. High liquidity in the options chain ensures that you can easily trade both puts and calls without incurring unnecessary costs.

Another excellent criterion for selecting stocks to use with The Wheel strategy is finding companies where you have a long-term bullish outlook but believe the stock is currently overpriced and likely to experience a pullback or correction. Traditional investing tactics would require you to sit on the sidelines and wait for the stock to drop to a price you consider fair before committing to a purchase. However, The Wheel offers a significant advantage in this scenario.

By selling cash-secured puts, you can commit to buying the stock at a price you believe is reasonable, while getting paid upfront through the option premium while you wait. If the stock drops to your desired level, you still keep the option premium and the shares will be assigned to you at the discounted price you agreed to. If the equity remains overpriced, the premium you collected remains as profit, and you can reevaluate or continue selling puts until your price target is met.

For instance, imagine you're bullish on a tech company that has strong growth potential but is currently trading at a price you feel is unsustainably high. While traditional investors might stay on the sidelines and hope for a correction, using The Wheel, you could sell puts at a strike price aligned with your valuation of the stock. If the price eventually drops, you'll acquire the shares at the level you wanted while also keeping the premiums earned during the waiting period.

This approach not only helps you avoid overpaying for stocks but also allows you to generate income while waiting for the right buying opportunity. It's a win-win scenario that blends the patience of value investing with the income-generating potential of options trading, making The Wheel an even more versatile and powerful strategy.

Tools for Stock Selection

One of the greatest advantages of thorough research is the ability to build a watchlist of reliable stocks that align with your trading strategy. By identifying and familiarizing yourself with a set of stocks that consistently meet your criteria, you can save time on future trades and profit repeatedly from the effort you've already invested. This allows you to focus on stocks with predictable behavior, making it easier to anticipate movements and plan trades.

Now, let's dive into some of the most valuable tools available to streamline your stock selection process.

Stock Screeners:

Stock screeners are invaluable tools for narrowing down the vast universe of stocks to a manageable list that meets your criteria. Platforms like Finviz, Yahoo Finance, and tools provided by your brokerage allow you to apply filters such as market capitalization, dividend yield, price-to-earnings (P/E) ratio, and historical or implied volatility.

For example, if you're looking for stable, income-generating stocks, you might filter for companies with high dividend yields and consistent earnings growth. On the other hand, if you're pursuing an options strategy that benefits from volatility, you could focus on stocks with high beta or implied volatility. Learn how to customize these filters based on your strategy to save time and find opportunities that align with your goals.

Industry Research:

Understanding the broader market and industry trends can help you make informed stock selections. Regularly reading financial news, analyst reports, and industry publications can provide insights into which sectors are thriving or facing challenges. For instance, during periods of economic growth, cyclical industries like consumer discretionary and technology may offer more opportunities. Conversely, defensive sectors such as utilities and healthcare might be more appealing during economic downturns. Leverage resources like Bloomberg, The Wall Street Journal, and industry-specific blogs to stay informed. Engaging in this research also helps you anticipate potential catalysts, such as regulatory changes or technological breakthroughs, that could impact your selected stocks.

Earnings Calendars:

Earnings announcements often lead to significant price movements, which can both create opportunities and introduce risks, depending on your strategy. Tools like Nasdaq's Earnings Calendar or the calendar available on your trading platform can help you track upcoming earnings dates. For options traders, this is particularly important, as implied volatility often spikes leading up to an earnings report, inflating option premiums. By being aware of these dates, you can decide whether to capitalize on the increased volatility or avoid the equity entirely to reduce risk. Understanding the typical price reactions of specific stocks during earnings can also enhance your decision-making.

Now, that you know how to identify quality stocks, let's look at each step in the The Wheel in detail.

Step 1: Cash-Secured Puts

The first step in The Wheel strategy is selling cash-secured puts. This means you sell put options on a stock and set aside enough cash to purchase 100 shares of the equity for each option contract you sell. This ensures you're financially prepared to fulfill your obligation if the stock price drops to the level where you've agreed to purchase it.

Here's how it works:

Select a Stock:

Start by choosing a stock you'd be comfortable owning for the long term. Refer back to the criteria we discussed earlier in this chapter, such as focusing on industries you understand, stocks with strong fundamentals, moderate and consistent volatility, and active options markets. These factors will help you identify high-quality candidates for this strategy.

Determine the Strike Price For Your Put:

Selecting the appropriate strike price is key to aligning the trade with your strategy and risk tolerance. In most cases, you'll choose a strike price below the current market price of the stock. This means you are agreeing to purchase shares at a discount relative to their current value, should the stock price drop to or below your chosen strike price. This approach ensures that you're acquiring shares at a price you consider favorable.

This basic setup is often used because it balances the desire to collect a meaningful premium with the potential to buy the stock at a lower price. However, as you gain experience and explore advanced strategies (discussed in later chapters), you'll learn how using higher strike prices in specific market conditions can create unique opportunities. For now, we'll focus on the foundational approach to keep things simple and straightforward.

Collect the Premium:

One of the immediate benefits of selling a put option is the premium you receive upon executing the trade. This premium is deposited directly into your account and is yours to keep, regardless of the trade's outcome. This upfront income serves two purposes:

- **Compensation for Risk**:
  By selling the put, you take on the obligation to potentially purchase the stock at the strike price. The premium acts as compensation for accepting this risk, ensuring you're paid for committing to this obligation.

- **Cost Basis Reduction:**
  If the stock price drops and you're assigned shares, the premium you collected effectively lowers your cost basis, providing you with an additional buffer against potential losses.

This dual benefit makes selling puts an attractive strategy for generating income and potentially acquiring stocks at a discount, while keeping your risk managed within the parameters you've set.

Example:

Let's say you're considering an equity which is currently trading at $50. You decide to sell a put with a strike price of $45, and you collect a premium of $2 per share ($200 per contract).

By selling a strike $45 put, you're agreeing to buy 100 shares at $45 per share if required. In exchange for making the agreement, you collect $200 up front.

If the equity stays above $45, the option will expire worthless and you will simply keep the $200 as compensation for agreeing to take on the obligation, even though you never had to follow through.

If the stock is trading below $45 when the option expires, or if the buyer exercises their right before the option expires, you will need to honor your agreement and purchase 100 shares for $45 each. The $2 premium you collected will effectively reduce your cost basis to $43 per share ($45 - $2).

For many people new to options trading, the concept of selling something you don't own, like a put option, can be confusing. A common question is, "Don't I need to buy a put before I can sell it to someone else?" Others view the obligation to buy shares as a downside they should avoid. To demystify these ideas, let's use an analogy: selling a put is a lot like being an insurance company selling coverage.

Insurance Analogy:

Think about your car insurance. You pay the insurance company a premium to keep your policy active for a specific period. In return, the company agrees to pay for damages to your car if something happens, like an accident, during that time. The insurance company doesn't own your car, but it assumes the risk of covering the cost of damages if a covered event occurs. If no accidents happen during the policy term, the company keeps the premium as profit without any further obligations.

Selling a put option works in a similar way. When you sell a put, you're essentially acting as the "insurer" for a stock. The buyer of the put pays you a premium for the promise that you will buy their shares at a predetermined price (the strike price) if the stock's value drops below that level. If the stock price remains above the strike price during the option's term, the contract expires worthless, and you keep the premium as your profit, just like an insurance company keeps the premium if no claim is filed.

If the stock price falls below the strike price, you fulfill your obligation by buying the stock at the agreed-upon price. This is comparable to the insurance company "paying out" on a claim. However, unlike an insurance company that must pay for a damaged car (which often has limited or no value), your "payout" is investing in shares of a stock you've carefully researched and believe has strong long-term potential.

Turning a Liability Into an Asset:

The key difference between selling car insurance and selling puts is that, as a put seller, you're not taking on a liability that depreciates or disappears after a claim. Instead, you're acquiring an asset, shares of stock, at a price you've carefully selected. This turns what some see as a risk into an opportunity. By owning a quality stock at a discounted price, you position yourself to benefit from potential future gains.

This obligation isn't a drawback; it's the heart of the strategy.

Some traders find it helpful to think of this process as "writing a put" rather than "selling a put." This terminology highlights that you're creating the contract that you intend to sell. Just like an insurance company drafts a policy and sells it to a customer, you're the one originating the put option. You are creating the contract, setting the terms, and agreeing to take on the associated obligations in exchange for the premium.

Calculating Your Return

When selling options, we use Return on Risk (ROR) instead of the more common Return on Investment (ROI) used in tradition investing. This is because the capital requirement for the trades are different from a typical investments. In traditional investing, ROI measures your return based on total gains compared to the total amount invested. However, when selling cash-secured puts you don't actually spend capital to enter the trade. In fact, you won't invest any capital at all unless you're assigned the stock. Instead, you set aside the cash to secure the trade so the capital is available if you are assigned shares. This means that in order to calculate your return accurately you use your maximum gain and compare that to the total cash reserved.

The formula for Return on Risk (ROR) for selling cash-secured puts is:

$$ROR = \frac{Premium\ Received}{Capital\ at\ Risk} \times 100$$

Let's break this down:

- **Premium Received:**
  The amount you collect for selling the put option. This is quoted on a per-share basis but applies to 100 shares for each contract sold.

- **Capital at Risk:**
  This is the agreed-upon price (strike price) multiplied by 100 shares per contract minus the premium you received. It represents the total amount of cash you need to reserve in your account to secure the trade.

$$Capital\ at\ Risk = (Strike\ Price - Premium) \times 100$$

Example Calculation:

Let's calculate the ROR from the earlier example:

- Current stock price: $50
- Strike price of the put: $45
- Premium received: $2 per share (or $200 for one contract)

The Capital at Risk is the amount you'd need to buy 100 shares of XYZ at $45, minus the credit you received for selling the put:

$$\textit{Capital at Risk} = (\$45 - \$2) \times 100 = \$4300$$

Now we can use this information to calculate the Return on Risk:

$$ROR = \frac{\$200}{\$4300} \times 100 = 4.65\%$$

This means you are earning a 4.65% return on the $4,300 of risk capital you reserved for the trade.

Why ROR Matters

ROR gives you a clear picture of the income potential of your cash-secured put trades relative to the capital you're committing. Since options contracts are time-sensitive, ROR also allows you to compare opportunities across different expiration dates. A 4.65% return over a one-month period is far more attractive than the same return over six months because the shorter duration lets you redeploy your capital more frequently.

Annualizing ROR

To compare ROR across trades with different expiration dates, you can annualize the return to see its potential over a year. The formula for annualized ROR is:

$$\textit{Annualized ROR} = \frac{ROR}{\textit{Days in the Trade}} \times 365$$

Assuming the example earlier used a put with a 30-day expiration:

$$\textit{Annualized ROR} = \frac{4.65}{30} \times 365 = 56.58\%$$

This shows that if you could replicate the same trade every 30 days, your annualized return on your risk capital could exceed 56%, demonstrating the compounding potential of The Wheel strategy, and why it outperforms traditional long-term investment strategies.

It's important to balance return with risk. Don't rely on ROR alone. Higher premiums often come with greater volatility, so you should consider the stock's fundamentals and your overall strategy goals when selecting trades. Remember that sustainable success with The Wheel strategy relies on thoughtful planning and disciplined execution. Don't take on more risk than is necessary to achieve your goals, and always prioritize consistent, manageable growth over the allure of quick, high-stakes profits.

Step 2: Selling Covered Calls

If you're assigned shares from selling cash-secured puts, congratulations! You now own shares of a stock you like, and you paid less than you would have if you bought the shares outright instead of selling the put! Now, it's time to move to the next step of The Wheel strategy: selling covered calls. This step allows you to generate additional income from your shares by deciding how much profit you are willing to accept before you're willing to sell your shares, and collect additional income until you reach it.

Collecting Rent on Your Shares

Investing in shares is a lot like investing in Real Estate. In both cases you purchase an asset with the expectation that the asset will appreciate over time. Can you imagine purchasing an apartment complex and letting it sit vacant? You could simply sit on the property and wait for its value to appreciate, but you would be missing out on a huge revenue source by not collecting rent. Renting out the apartments generates consistent income while you continue to own the property and benefit from its potential long-term appreciation. Think of selling covered calls like renting out your shares to generate additional profits.

When you own shares of a stock, you could simply hold them and wait for the price to rise, but selling covered calls allows you to "collect rent" in the form of option premiums. This provides steady income from your investment while still allowing you to benefit from stock appreciation up to the strike price of your call. The analogy isn't perfect, because you can rent out an apartment without agreeing to sell it, but the core idea is the same: generate income from an asset you own.

How Covered Calls Work

Select a Strike Price:

Choose a strike price above your cost basis (the price you paid for the stock). This ensures that if the stock is called away, you will sell it for a profit.

Example:

If you own shares with a cost basis of $43 per share, you might sell a call with a strike price of $50. This means you agree to sell your shares at $50 if the stock price rises above that level.

Select an Expiration Date:

Short-term calls (1-4 weeks) are often ideal for maximizing time decay while maintaining flexibility.

- Shorter expirations allow you to adjust more frequently based on market conditions and can result in higher annualized returns.

- Longer-term calls can be used if you prefer a more hands-off approach, but the premium received is spread over a longer period, reducing your flexibility to respond to changing prices.

Collect the Premium:

When you sell the call, you receive a premium upfront. This income is yours to keep regardless of whether the stock is called away.

Example:

Let's continue from the previous example to show you how selling covered calls fits naturally into The Wheel strategy and generates income while lowering your cost basis.

Step 1: Sell a Put

Let's say you're considering an equity which is currently trading at $50. You decide to sell a put with a strike price of $45, and you collect a premium of $2 per share ($200 for one contract). The stock then drops to $44, and you are assigned 100 shares at the $45 strike price.

Because you collected $2 per share in premium from selling the put, your cost basis is reduced to $43 per share:

$$Cost\ Basis = Strike\ Price - Premium$$

$$Cost\ Basis = \$45 - \$2 = \$43$$

You now own 100 shares with a cost basis of $43 per share.

Step 2: Sell Covered Calls

With 100 shares in hand, you sell a covered call with a $50 strike price and collect $1.50 per share in premium ($150 for one contract). This further reduces your cost basis:

$$New\ Cost\ Basis = Previous\ Cost\ Basis - Covered\ Call\ Premium$$
$$New\ Cost\ Basis = \$43 - \$1.50 = \$41.50$$

Now your effective cost basis is $41.50 per share, providing a buffer against further potential downside in the stock price.

Scenario 1: The Stock Rises Above $50

If the stock is trading above $50 at expiration—for instance, $51—your shares will be called away. This means you sell your stock at the agreed-upon price of $50 per share, as specified in the covered call option. By selling the call, you agreed to cap your gains at $50 per share in exchange for the premium you collected upfront. While you forfeit any additional gains above $50, the trade still results in a significant profit:

$$Profit\ per\ share = Strike\ Price - New\ Cost\ Basis$$
$$Profit\ per\ share = \$50 - \$41.50 = \$8.50$$

Since you own 100 shares, your total profit is:

$$\$8.50 \times 100 = \$850$$

This total profit includes three components:

- **Stock Appreciation:**
  $5 per share from the stock's rise between the initial put strike price ($45) and the covered call strike price ($50).
- **Premium from the Put Option (Step 1 of The Wheel):**
  $2 per share collected when you initially sold the put option.

- **Premium from the Call Option (Step 2 of The Wheel):** $1.50 per share collected when you sold the covered call option.

By adding these together, your total profit per share is $8.50, or $850 per contract. This demonstrates how The Wheel strategy combines income from premiums with capital appreciation to maximize returns in a structured and methodical way.

Comparison with a Traditional Investor:

Some traders feel frustrated when their shares are called away, thinking they're missing out on potential upside. While it's true that the seller forfeits gains above the covered call's strike price, it's important to consider the broader picture. Later in the book, we'll discuss ways to adapt trades to capitalize on additional bullishness. For now, let's compare the performance of this trade to that of a traditional buy-and-hold investor to highlight how much stronger the returns can be, even with the "missed" $1 of upside.

If a traditional investor had purchased the stock outright at $50 and sold it at $51, their profit would be limited to $1 per share, or $100 for 100 shares.

In contrast, The Wheel strategy delivers a significantly higher profit of $8.50 per share ($850 for 100 shares). For a buy-and-hold investor to match this return, the stock would need to appreciate by more than 17% and reach $58.50 by the time the call expires—a scenario that's far less common.

By combining stock appreciation with option premiums, The Wheel strategy generates multiple streams of income, making it a more consistent and versatile approach that outperforms traditional investing methods in all but the most exceptionally bullish cases.

Scenario 2: The Stock Stays Below $50

If the stock does not rise above $50 before the covered call expires, your obligation to sell your shares at $50 becomes irrelevant. The buyer has no incentive to exercise the option because they can purchase the stock for less than $50 on the open market. As a result, the call will expire worthless.

Even though the option expires, you still keep the $150 premium you collected when you sold the call option. Additionally, you benefit from any stock appreciation during the period up to the call's strike price. Let's say the stock is trading at $48 when the call expires. Here's how the outcome breaks down:

- **Premium Collected:**
  You were assigned shares in Step 1 at $45 per share, but the $2 premium collected from the cash-secured put lowered your effective cost basis to $43. The additional $1.50 per share premium from selling the covered call further reduces your cost basis from $43 to $41.50.

- **Stock Appreciation:**
  With the stock price rising to $48, you achieve a $6.50 per share gain. This is calculated as the difference between your cost basis ($41.50) and the stock's new price ($48).

$$Profit\ per\ Share = Current\ Stock\ Price - New\ Cost\ Basis$$

$$Profit\ per\ Share = \$48 - \$41.50 = \$6.50$$

With 100 shares, your total gain is:

$$\$6.50 \times 100 = \$650$$

In this scenario, your shares were not called away, so you retain ownership of the stock. This positions you to continue generating additional income by repeating the process. You can sell another covered call, collect another premium, and continue this cycle until your shares are eventually called away. Each iteration of this strategy adds to your overall returns, combining stock appreciation with premium income to steadily build wealth over time.

Comparison with a Traditional Investor:

If a traditional investor had purchased the stock when it was trading at $50, they would have experienced a loss when the stock dropped to $44. Even though the equity later recovered to $48, they would still be down by $2 per share ($48 - $50).

In contrast, thanks to the premiums collected along the way, your cost basis with The Wheel strategy was reduced to $41.50 per share, resulting in a $6.50 per share gain when the stock reached $48.

Moreover, The Wheel strategy would still have been profitable as long as the stock price remained above your cost basis of $41.50. This means if the stock had continued to fall, you would have maintained a profit, though it would have been smaller, until it broke below your cost basis.

Later in the book, we'll discuss advanced techniques to add downside protection, helping to safeguard against bearish moves. However, even with this basic setup, The Wheel will always outperform traditional buy-and-hold methods in bear markets. This is because each step in The Wheel reduces your cost basis, mitigating the impact of declining prices and preserving profitability in ways that static long-term investments cannot achieve.

Addressing the Fear of Missing Out

When selling a covered call, you are essentially exchanging the potential for future profits for immediate, tangible income. One of the biggest concerns for new traders is the fear of missing out (FOMO) if the stock's future potential turns out to be greater than the profit they locked in.

For example, new traders often worry, "What if the stock skyrockets and I miss out on all the gains above the strike price?" This is a valid concern, but understanding how to approach this situation can help you make more confident decisions. While advanced strategies to address this will be covered later in the book, let's explore this concern from a practical perspective.

A stock breaking through your strike price is a good thing!

If the stock surpasses your covered call strike price, it's not a reason for regret—it's a reason to celebrate! Why? Because you've achieved the maximum profit possible for that trade. You've captured gains from the stock's appreciation up to the strike price and collected the call premium as additional income.

This is why selecting the right strike price is critical. The strike price determines your maximum profit, so it's important to choose a level that aligns with your goals. Here's how you can approach it:

Maximizing Potential Appreciation:

If you want to retain your shares and leave room for the stock to appreciate further, choose a strike price well above where you expect the stock to trade before the option expires. While this approach reduces the premium you collect, it allows you to participate in more upside if the stock rises significantly. This strategy works best in bullish environments or when you believe the stock has strong upward potential. But you should still be willing to part with the shares at this level if the equity surprises you.

Prioritizing Consistent Income:

If your focus is on generating reliable income and locking in gains, consider choosing a strike price closer to the current stock price. This maximizes the premium collected upfront but caps your potential gains at a lower level. It's a trade-off: you're giving up some "theoretical" future profit in exchange for higher immediate returns.

Reframing Missed Opportunities

It's also important to reframe how you view the outcome of selling a covered call. If your shares are called away, this is not a failure but a success. Here's why:

- **What You Gained:**
  You earned income from the call premium and realized profits from the stock's appreciation up to the strike price. **This is a profitable, successful trade.**

- **What You "Lost":**
  Nothing! Any gains above the strike price that weren't captured are not losses. They're simply unrealized opportunities, and they don't impact the profitability of the trade you executed. Focusing on the profits you achieved, rather than on the hypothetical "what could have been," helps you maintain a positive perspective.

Covered Calls Are a Tool, Not a Requirement.

If you believe a stock is about to rally—perhaps due to an upcoming earnings report, a product launch, or another catalyst—you don't need to sell a covered call immediately. You can temporarily hold your shares without selling calls to allow for greater upside. Once the stock reaches a resistance level, you can sell calls to lock in gains while continuing to generate income.

This flexibility ensures you remain in control of your trades and can adjust your approach based on your expectations about the stock's future performance.

The Power of Repetition and Compounding

Even if a stock rallies far beyond your covered call strike price, The Wheel strategy is cyclical, allowing you to continue generating returns. After your shares are called away, you simply return to Step 1 and sell cash-secured puts, either on the same stock or another equity you're interested in.

This ongoing cycle of selling puts, acquiring shares, and selling covered calls creates a compounding effect. Over time, the small "missed opportunities" are far outweighed by the consistent income and wealth-building potential of the strategy as a whole.

By focusing on the long-term benefits of The Wheel strategy, you can overcome the fear of missing out and make confident, informed decisions that align with your financial goals.

Calculating ROI on a Covered Call

To calculate the return on a covered call trade, we return to using Return on Investment (ROI), because capital is now fully invested in the position through stock ownership. Your ROI calculation will vary depending on whether the shares are called away at the strike price or the covered call expires worthless.

The formula is:

$$ROI = \frac{Stock\ Price\ or\ Strike\ Price - Cost\ Basis}{Cost\ Basis} \times 100$$

Here's how to apply this formula step-by-step:

Let's assume the following:

- **Cost Basis:** $41.50 (adjusted for premiums from previous trades).
- **Covered Call Strike Price:** $50

Scenario 1: The Stock Is Called Away

If the stock rises above the strike price, your shares will be called away, meaning you sell them at the agreed strike price of $50. In this case, the value used in the ROI calculation is the strike price:

$$ROI = \frac{Strike\ Price - Cost\ Basis}{Cost\ Basis} \times 100$$

$$ROI = \frac{\$50 - \$41.50}{\$41.50} \times 100 = \frac{8.50}{41.50} \times 100 = 20.48\%$$

Using this formula, the ROI is 20.48%, which includes the profit from the premium collected and the appreciation of the stock up to the strike price. This represents the maximum return for this trade setup.

Scenario 2: The Stock Remains Below the Strike Price

If the stock price rises to $48 but does not exceed the strike price, the covered call expires worthless, and you retain your shares. In this case, the value used in the ROI calculation is the current stock price of $48:

$$ROI = \frac{Current\ Stock\ Price - Cost\ Basis}{Cost\ Basis} \times 100$$

$$ROI = \frac{48 - 41.50}{41.50} \times 100 = \frac{6.50}{41.50} \times 100 = 15.66\%$$

Here, the ROI is 15.66%, reflecting a partial profit from the stock's appreciation and the premium collected. While this return is lower than if the stock had been called away, it still represents a profitable trade, and the total return can continue to go up as sell more covered calls.

Key Points to Remember When Calculating ROI:

- **If the Stock is Above Your Strike Price:**
  Use the **strike price** in the calculation, as this is the price at which your shares are sold.

- **If the Stock is Below Your Strike Price:**

Use the **current stock price** in the calculation, as it reflects the stocks value when the option expires worthless.

- **Adjust for Cost Basis:**
  Incorporate all premiums collected in your cost basis to ensure the ROI accurately capture the true profitability of the trade.

Annualized ROI

Annualized ROI allows you to assess the potential performance of a trade if it could be repeated consistently over the course of a year. This provides a standardized way to compare the profitability of trades with different timeframes and highlights the compounding potential of The Wheel strategy.

The formula for calculating annualized ROI is:

$$Annualized\ ROI = \frac{ROI}{Days\ in\ the\ Trade} \times 365$$

Let's apply this to the two scenarios discussed earlier, assuming a 30-day expiration for the covered call:

Scenario 1: The Stock Is Called Away

If the stock rises above the strike price and your shares are called away, the annualized ROI can be calculated as:

$$Annualized\ ROI = \frac{20.48}{30} \times 365 = 249.17\%$$

In this scenario, the annualized return exceeds 249%, showing the immense compounding potential of repeating such trades consistently over a year. This high return combines the premium collected with the maximum profit from stock appreciation up to the strike price.

Scenario 2: The Stock Remains Below the Strike Price

If the stock price rises to $48 and the covered call expires worthless, the annualized ROI can be calculated as:

$$Annualized\ ROI = \frac{15.66}{30} \times 365 = 190.53\%$$

In this case, the annualized return is still substantial, reflecting the combined benefits of partial stock appreciation and the premium collected. Even without shares being called away, the consistent income generated by selling calls significantly enhances profitability.

These calculations demonstrate the power of The Wheel strategy to deliver exceptional returns. By collecting premiums and leveraging stock appreciation in a systematic, repeatable process, The Wheel often outperforms traditional buy-and-hold investment strategies.

Step 3: Repeat the Cycle

The true strength of The Wheel strategy lies in its flexibility and cyclical nature. After completing Step 1 (selling cash-secured puts) and Step 2 (selling covered calls), you seamlessly return to Step 1 to begin the process anew. Each cycle generates income through premiums, reduces your cost basis, and positions you to profit in various market conditions.

Importantly, The Wheel is not a rigid formula, it can be tailored to your specific goals. For instance, you can choose to skip Step 2 and hold the acquired stock for long-term appreciation. Let's explore how the cycle repeats and ways you can adjust the strategy to fit your objectives.

Repeating Step 1: Selling Cash-Secured Puts

If your cash-secured puts expire worthless because the stock didn't drop below your strike price, you can simply repeat Step 1 and sell more cash-secured puts. At this stage, it's essential to assess the current stock price and market conditions to determine your next move.

If the Stock Price Appreciated

If the stock price has risen since your last trade, consider selling puts at a higher strike price to capitalize on the stock's upward movement.

Adjusting your strike prices higher as the equity moves higher will allow you to target similar or higher premiums. However, keep in mind that a higher strike price increases the amount of capital required to secure the position. Carefully evaluate your position sizing and risk tolerance to ensure it aligns with your overall strategy.

If the Stock Price Declined

If the stock price has fallen, adjust your strike price lower to reflect the new price levels and maintain a margin of safety.

By lowering your strike price, you ensure that you're only assigned shares at a price you're comfortable with, protecting yourself against further downside risk. This approach also helps you maintain flexibility in adapting to changing market conditions.

Evaluating New Opportunities

Repeating Step 1 doesn't mean you're obligated to stick with the same stock. The Wheel strategy allows you to evaluate other equities that meet your selection criteria. Diversifying across multiple stocks or sectors can reduce risk and enhance your long-term profitability.

A Dynamic and Adaptable Strategy

The Wheel strategy's adaptability is what makes it so powerful. By assessing the stock price and market conditions at each stage, you can adjust your approach to optimize returns while managing risk. Whether you choose to stick with the same stock, lower your strike price, or explore new opportunities, each cycle of The Wheel builds on the last, compounding your income and reducing your cost basis over time.

Repeating Step 2: Selling Covered Calls

If you're assigned shares from Step 1, you'll move to Step 2 and sell covered calls. If your covered call expires worthless and your shares are not called away, you repeat Step 2 until the shares are eventually sold. Each time you return to Step 2, it's important to assess the stock's performance and adjust your approach accordingly to optimize returns.

If the Stock Is Slowly Appreciating

When the stock price is gradually rising, consider selling calls with a higher strike price to capture more of the appreciation while still earning a premium.

By selecting a higher strike price you give the stock more room to grow, allowing you to participate in additional upside. While premiums at higher strike prices may be smaller, this approach balances income generation with the opportunity for greater capital gains if the stock continues to rise.

If the Stock Is Flat or Declining

In a stagnant or declining market, selling calls closer to your cost basis can help maximize premium income while providing some protection against further losses.

By selling calls near or at your cost basis, you generate higher premiums that can offset potential losses if the stock's value continues to decline. While this approach caps your upside at a lower level, it ensures consistent income in less favorable market conditions.

Adjusting Expiration Dates

Each time you repeat Step 2, you also have the flexibility to adjust the expiration dates for your covered calls:

- **Shorter-Term Options:**
  These allow for more frequent adjustments and quick premium collection, making them ideal if you expect short-term price stability or small movements.

- **Longer-Term Options:**
  These provide higher upfront premiums and require less frequent management, making them suitable if you anticipate a stable or slow-moving stock over a longer period.

Your choice of expiration will depend on your market outlook and income goals. Shorter-term options may align with a more active approach, while longer-term options can reduce transaction frequency and simplify management.

Completing the Cycle

Once your shares are called away, the cycle is complete, and you're ready to return to Step 1. This continuous process of selling cash-secured puts and covered calls allows you to systematically generate income and grow your portfolio while adapting to evolving market conditions. The beauty of The Wheel strategy lies in its ability to repeat this cycle over and over, creating a compounding effect that builds wealth steadily over time.

Key Benefits of Repetition

1. **Compounding Gains:**
   Each completed cycle adds to your overall profitability. The premiums collected during each step either lower your cost basis or provide immediate income. Over time, this creates a compounding effect, amplifying your returns with every cycle.

2. **Flexibility:**
   The Wheel strategy is highly adaptable. You can adjust strike prices, expiration dates, or even switch to trading different equities based on your goals and changing market conditions. This flexibility ensures the strategy remains effective regardless of the market.

3. **Resilience in Volatile Markets:**
   The consistent income from selling premiums acts as a buffer against adverse price movements, helping you navigate volatility with confidence.

4. **More Control Over Your Portfolio:**
   The Wheel strategy empowers you to take an active role in managing your investments, the strategy is designed to align with your preferences and objectives.

Repetition is where the true power of The Wheel strategy lies. By cycling through Steps 1 and 2 or skipping Step 2 when holding a stock long-term, you maintain the flexibility to adapt to your goals while steadily building wealth.

This adaptability makes The Wheel both rewarding and easy to tailor to your specific financial needs, establishing it as a cornerstone of smart options trading.

By focusing on quality stocks and strategically using options to lower your cost basis, you mitigate some of the inherent risks of stock ownership. Additionally, the consistent income generated through premiums not only enhances your gains but also provides a buffer against losses elsewhere in your portfolio. Over time, this approach creates a robust framework for wealth generation, regardless of market conditions.

CHAPTER 3

TAXES AND FEES

WHAT EVERY TRADER SHOULD KNOW

TAXES AND FEES ARE an unavoidable part of trading, and their impact on profitability should never be underestimated. Understanding how they work is crucial to successfully implementing The Wheel strategy and optimizing your returns. This chapter provides a general overview of key considerations, including broker fees, capital gains, and tax-advantaged accounts. It's important to note that Scholarly Mind Creations, LLC is not a tax professional, and this information is not a substitute for professional guidance. Always consult a qualified tax professional in your area to understand how these principles apply to your specific situation.

Broker Fees and Costs

Trading fees vary widely among brokers, and understanding their impact is crucial to optimizing your profitability. While it might seem helpful to provide a list of brokers and their fees, I feel it's important for traders to do their own research for several reasons:

1. **Fee Structures Change Frequently:** Brokerage fees are not static. Brokers regularly adjust their pricing models to stay competitive, and any list of fees provided today could become outdated in a matter of months.

2. **Mergers and Acquisitions:** Brokers are occasionally bought, sold, or merged. These changes can result in significant alterations to fee structures, platform features, and service offerings, again causing any list to become outdated.

3. **Global Variation:** Options trading is a global activity, and not all brokers service the same regions. The brokers available in one country may not operate in another, and this availability can change over time. Additionally, fees and regulatory requirements may differ based on location, making a one-size-fits-all list impractical.

4. **Personal Preferences:** Finally, the "best" broker often depends on your trading strategy, preferences, and priorities. Some traders may prioritize low fees, while others value advanced trading tools, customer service, or educational resources and are willing to pay higher fees for those resources.

For these reasons, it's essential for traders to invest the time and effort to research brokers themselves. Look for brokers that align with your strategy and region, and compare their fee structures, available tools, and overall reputation to find the best fit for your needs. This approach ensures you're getting the most accurate and up-to-date information for your unique situation.

That being said, here are some of the fees and fee structures you will find:

Assignment Fees:

Some brokers charge an "assignment fee" when shares are assigned, which can eat into your profits. For example, if you sell a put that gets assigned, your broker may charge an assignment fee when those shares are added to your account. These fees can be a flat fee or based on the number of shares. Assignment fees often have a higher impact on small trades, so it's critical to include them in your cost-basis calculations to determine if the trade is truly profitable.

Transaction Costs:

Brokers differ in how they charge fees for opening, closing, or letting options expire worthless:

- **Per-Contract Fees**: Many brokers charge a per-contract fee for every options contract when a trade is opened, others charge fees for both opening and closing positions. Most have no fees for expiring contracts. This means fees will increase or decrease as your position size changes.

- **Flat Monthly Fees**: Some brokers offer a flat monthly fee structure, which may be beneficial for high-volume traders but less cost-effective for less active traders or those trading smaller position sizes.

- **Equity Trade Fees**: Buying and selling shares may also incur fees, which are often small but can add up quickly for active traders.

Over time, these costs can erode returns, especially for traders executing a large number of smaller trades. When evaluating brokers, consider not only the per-trade costs but also the overall structure and how it aligns with your trading frequency and style.

Tax Considerations

Taxes play a significant role in determining your overall trading profitability. By understanding how gains are classified and how losses can be used strategically, you can optimize your tax outcomes while staying compliant with IRS regulations.

The way your trades are taxed depends partially on the holding period of the shares and the nature of the income. Options premiums and stock sales may fall under different categories, making it essential to understand how each impacts your tax obligations.

Short-Term Capital Gains:

If you hold a stock for less than a year before selling it, any gains will be taxed as ordinary income, which often comes with a higher tax rate. Premiums collected from selling options, such as cash-secured puts or covered calls, also typically fall into this category, as they are considered short-term income.

Long-Term Capital Gains:

Holding assigned shares for more than a year before selling qualifies you for the lower long-term capital gains tax rate. This distinction can make a significant difference in your after-tax returns, particularly if you frequently allow puts or calls to be assigned.

Tax-Loss Harvesting

Tax-loss harvesting is a strategy that involves selling securities at a loss to offset taxable gains elsewhere in your portfolio.

- **How It Works:**
  If you realize a gain from one trade, you can sell underperforming securities at a loss to offset that gain. For example, if you make a $5,000 profit on a successful covered call trade but also have $3,000 in unrealized losses from shares in another stock, selling the losing stock can reduce your taxable gain to $2,000.
- **Key Considerations:**
  - **Wash Sale Rule Interaction:** Be careful to avoid repurchasing the same stock within the wash sale window, as this would disallow the loss.
  - **Offset Ordinary Income:** In addition to offsetting capital gains, you can use up to $3,000 of net losses to reduce ordinary income. Excess losses can be carried forward to future tax years.
  - **End-of-Year Strategy:** Tax-loss harvesting is often used at the end of the year to minimize tax liability, but you can apply it anytime you realize gains.

Wash Sale Rules

The IRS's wash sale rule prevents you from claiming a tax deduction for a loss if you purchase the same or a substantially identical security within 30 days before or after the sale.

Impact on Wheel Traders:
Frequent re-entry into trades on the same stock can trigger the wash sale rule. For instance, if you sell a stock at a loss and then re-enter a new put position

on the same equity within the wash sale window, the initial loss may not be deductible.

Tips to Avoid Wash Sales:

- **Space Out Trades:**
  Allow at least 30 days before re-entering a position in the same stock after selling the shares at a loss to avoid triggering the rule.
- **Use Different Securities:**
  Diversify your trades by selecting different stocks for your options positions.
- **Keep Accurate Records:**
  Detailed tracking of your trades ensures compliance with wash sale regulations.

Tax-Advantaged Accounts

Tax-advantaged accounts, such as IRAs or 401(k)s, provide a valuable way to shield your trades from immediate taxation. While these accounts come with certain restrictions, they offer opportunities for compounding gains and long-term growth.

Benefits:

In a tax-advantaged account, you don't need to worry about the distinction between short-term and long-term gains, or even about wash sale rules. Profits can be reinvested in full, accelerating portfolio growth through compounding. For traders focused on long-term strategies, this tax-deferral mechanism can result in significantly higher net returns over time.

Drawbacks:

While tax-advantaged accounts have their benefits, they also come with limitations:

- **No Margin**: Most retirement accounts do not allow trading on margin, which can limit the flexibility of strategies like The Wheel.
- **Restricted Trades**: Certain high-risk trades, such as selling naked calls, are prohibited in retirement accounts.
- **Early Withdrawal Penalties**: Funds withdrawn before retirement age may be subject to penalties and taxes, making these accounts less suitable for traders relying on income generation in the short term.

Practical Tips for Managing Taxes and Fees

1. **Consult a Tax Professional**
   Tax laws are complex and vary by location. A tax professional can help you ensure you remain compliant with all regulations.
2. **Keep Detailed Records**
   Accurate tracking of every trade, including premiums, assignments, and sales, is essential for accurate tax reporting and identifying potential deductions.
3. **Consider Tax Implications When Planning Trades**
   Be mindful of the holding period for assigned shares and the timing of gains or losses to optimize your tax position.
4. **Account for Fees in Profit Calculations**
   Always include broker fees and assignment costs when evaluating the profitability of a trade. Even small fees can compound over time and impact your bottom line.

CHAPTER 4

ADVANCED STRATEGIES FOR TRADING THE WHEEL

UNLOCKING THE SECRETS TO MAXIMIZE RETURNS

NOW THAT WE'VE COVERED the foundational mechanics of The Wheel strategy, you're equipped with the tools to generate consistent income and build wealth by selling cash-secured puts and covered calls. These simple tools provides a straightforward and effective framework that works in virtually any market condition.

But what if you're ready to take your trading to the next level?

For traders seeking to enhance their returns and optimize their strategies, there are advanced techniques that build on The Wheel's core principles. These strategies not only open the door to higher potential profits but also introduce new ways to manage risk, fine-tune your trades, and adapt to changing market conditions.

In the chapters ahead, we'll explore topics like: using margin to leverage your account for higher returns, mastering time decay, using the Greeks to fine-tune your trades, dividend risk with covered calls, advanced strike price selection, adapting the Wheel to different market conditions to improve returns and reduce risks, and how reinvesting premiums and compounding growth can turn The Wheel into a cornerstone of your long-term financial strategy.

We'll begin with a powerful tool that can amplify your returns: using margin. While margin trading can free up capital and increase your leverage, it also introduces unique risks that must be carefully managed. Let's dive into how margin works, its benefits, and the potential pitfalls to avoid as you incorporate it into your Wheel strategy.

Chapter 5

Margin Trading and the Wheel

Risks and Rewards for Advanced Traders

When trading options, some traders choose to sell naked puts on margin rather than securing the trade with cash. This approach requires a smaller upfront commitment, which can significantly amplify potential returns. However, it also comes with heightened risks, and when mismanaged, it can lead to catastrophic losses.

What is Margin?

Margin is borrowed capital provided by your broker that allows you to trade with leverage. This means your broker essentially lends you money, charging you interest on the loan, so you can place trades without having to fully set aside the capital at risk. For options traders, this leverage allows greater flexibility, but it also introduces additional risks.

When you sell a naked put on margin, instead of reserving the full amount of cash needed to buy the shares at the agreed price, your broker only requires you to put up a fraction of the total amount. This reduced collateral requirement frees up funds in your account, enabling you to open additional trades or invest in other opportunities.

The Appeal and Risks of Margin

The reduced collateral requirement might seem appealing because it can amplify your rate of return. In the earlier example, if selling a strike $45 cash-secured put and collecting $2 per share of premium required $4,300 in collateral to generate a $200 profit. If you could place the same trade on margin, only setting aside $1,000 for the same profit (ignoring interest charges) this would increase your return from 4.65% to 20%. However, this reduction in reserved funds does not reduce the actual risk of the trade.

The fundamental risk in selling naked puts is that you are obligated to buy the stock if its price falls below the agreed-upon level. This obligation exists regardless of whether the put is cash-secured or traded on margin. If the stock drops sharply, the amount required to fulfill this obligation remains the same, and trading on margin may leave you underprepared to meet that obligation.

The Margin Call: When Things Go Wrong

If the stock price falls below the strike price and you don't have enough funds set aside to purchase the shares, your broker will issue a margin call. This is essentially a demand to immediately deposit additional funds into your account to cover the increased risk.

Failing to meet a margin call can trigger severe consequences. The broker's loss mitigation team may step in and begin liquidating other positions in your account to cover the shortfall. This liquidation is often done quickly, at market prices, without regard for your broader investment strategy, and it can result in substantial losses.

For example:

- **Cash-Secured Scenario:**
  If you sell a strike $45 put and collect $2 per share of premium, and the stock drops to $40, you have the full $4,300 set aside to buy the shares. While your portfolio may show a paper loss, you can still take ownership of the stock without any immediate disruption.

- **Margin Scenario:**
  If the same stock drops to $40 and you sold the put on margin, only putting $1,000 of the risk capital up front, you would still need the full $4,300 to cover your obligation to buy the shares. If your account lacks the additional $3,300, your broker will demand the funds. If you cannot immediately deposit the funds, your broker will cover the shortfall by liquidating other positions in your account, potentially at unfavorable prices.

Balancing Opportunity with Risk

Margin can provide flexibility and enhance returns, but it also magnifies potential losses, making it a tool that must be handled with care. While the allure of leveraging your account to amplify profits is tempting, it's crucial to remember that margin is not "free money" or "house money." Instead, it's a loan from your broker, one that comes with the potential for significant financial consequences if mismanaged.

The ability to trade on margin is a double-edged sword. On one hand, it offers the potential for higher returns by allowing traders to allocate less capital per trade and open more positions. On the other hand, it exposes traders to amplified risks. When trades move against you, the consequences are far more severe than they would be with cash-secured positions. To succeed, traders must use margin strategically and maintain a disciplined approach to risk management.

A Cautionary Tale: Mark's Story

Mark was a trader who started out cautiously, selling cash-secured puts. At first, he followed a disciplined approach, ensuring he had enough capital set aside to cover his obligations if assigned shares. Over time, however, Mark became overconfident. Seeking to maximize his returns, he began selling naked puts on margin.

Initially, everything went smoothly. Mark collected significant premiums, and his account balance grew rapidly. The returns from his margin trades far exceeded what he had earned with cash-secured positions, and this success only reinforced his confidence.

Then, in early 2020, the market experienced a sharp and unexpected downturn due to the COVID-19 pandemic. Stock prices plummeted seemingly overnight, and Mark's positions turned against him. One stock he had sold puts on dropped 40% in a single day, triggering his obligation to buy 1,000 shares at the agreed price. As the market continued to decline, similar obligations were triggered on his other positions.

Mark didn't have enough available funds to cover these obligations, and his broker issued a margin call, demanding he deposit additional capital immediately.

Unable to meet the margin requirements, Mark's broker began liquidating his remaining positions to cover the shortfall. This liquidation happened rapidly and at market prices, locking in massive losses.

By the time the dust settled, Mark's account had been wiped out. Years of profits were gone, and he was left with nothing but regret. When Mark eventually sought advice from me, it was too late, his overextension on margin had completely eroded his trading account.

Key Takeaways

Mark's story illustrates the dangers of trading on margin without proper risk management. While the potential for higher returns is enticing, it's essential to remain vigilant and avoid overextending yourself. Here are some lessons to keep in mind:

- **Limit Leverage:**
  Avoid using your full margin capacity. Just because you can open multiple positions doesn't mean you should. Always leave room in your account for unexpected market movements.

- **Prepare for the Worst:**
  Always consider the potential downside of every trade. If the stock dropped significantly, would you have enough capital to fulfill your obligation? If not, reconsider the trade or adjust your position size.

- **Diversify and Avoid Overconcentration:**
  Don't concentrate too much of your margin or capital in a single stock or sector. Diversification can help mitigate losses when one position moves against you.

- **Have an Exit Plan:**
  Know when to cut your losses. If a stock moves against you, consider closing the position early instead of waiting for a margin call.

- **Respect the Power of Margin:**
  Treat margin as a tool for responsible leverage, not as an opportunity to overreach. Its power can work for you or against you, depending on how you manage it.

By learning from cautionary tales like Mark's and maintaining a disciplined approach, you can use margin strategically without falling into the trap of overextension. The key is to balance opportunity with risk, ensuring that every decision you make is aligned with your financial goals.

Chapter 6

Adapting to Market Conditions

Customizing The Wheel to Fit Bullish and Bearish Trends

The Wheel strategy is inherently flexible, making it a valuable tool in any market environment. However, to maximize its effectiveness, you must adapt your approach to align with prevailing market conditions. This chapter provides practical guidance on tailoring The Wheel to thrive in bull, bear, and sideways markets.

Navigating Bull Markets: Maximizing Gains with The Wheel Strategy

The Wheel strategy is a powerful tool for generating consistent income in various market conditions, but its traditional structure inherently caps your upside potential in bull markets. Both the cash-secured put and the covered call have predefined upper limits, beyond which they stop generating profits. In a bull market, this cap can feel restrictive, as stocks often experience sustained growth, leaving traders wondering if they're leaving money on the table.

Advanced traders, however, can adapt The Wheel to capture more of the additional upside while still maintaining the strategy's core principles.

Before diving into adjustments, it's essential to understand how The Wheel caps profits:

- **Cash-Secured Puts:** The maximum profit is limited to the premium collected, regardless of how high the stock price climbs above the strike price.
- **Covered Calls:** If the stock price rises above the strike price of the call, your shares are called away, and any further appreciation is forfeited. This structure ensures steady income but can limit your ability to fully capitalize on strong bullish trends.

Adjusting Cash-Secured Puts for Bull Markets

In a bull market, where stocks are expected to rise steadily, traders can adjust their cash-secured put strategy to capture higher premiums and optimize returns.

Raising the Strike Price:

Selling puts closer to the current stock price, or even slightly in-the-money (ITM), can increase the premium collected, as these options have higher extrinsic value and may include some intrinsic value as well.

How it Works:

As the strike price moves closer to at-the-money (ATM), the extrinsic value reaches its peak, reflecting the higher uncertainty about where the stock price will go. If you sell a slightly ITM put, you capture this maximum extrinsic value and some intrinsic value as well, creating a larger upfront premium. If the stock continues to rise, the intrinsic and extrinsic value diminishes, quickly and the option price drops, enabling you to close the position profitably or let it expire worthless.

Considerations:

This approach works best if you are comfortable owning the shares, as an ITM put has a higher chance of assignment if the stock moves sideways or reverses.

Sell Puts with Longer Expirations, With the Intention of Closing Early:

Longer-term options naturally carry more extrinsic value because they account for a greater potential range of price movements over the extended time frame. Buyers are willing to pay a premium for this additional opportunity. Although longer-term options experience slower time decay compared to shorter-term options, a bullish move in the underlying stock can rapidly decrease their extrinsic value, even if the option has substantial time remaining.

How It Works:

As the stock price rises further above the strike price of the put, the market perceives a lower probability of the option being assigned. With this diminished assignment risk, the option's value decreases sharply, causing the premium to drop, even if the expiration date is weeks or months away. This phenomenon allows traders to profit not just from time decay but also from favorable price action in the underlying stock.

Repeat the Process:

Rather than waiting for short-term puts to expire worthless, this strategy enables you to lock in higher profits and redeploy your capital into new trades. By consistently selling longer-term puts and closing them after a rapid reduction in premium, you can often achieve two to three times the profits compared to relying solely on short-term puts.

Adjusting Covered Calls for Bull Markets

In bullish markets, covered calls can be adjusted to take advantage of rising stock prices while still generating income. The traditional approach of selling at-the-money or slightly out-of-the-money calls may limit your ability to fully capitalize on the upward momentum of a strong market.

Use Higher Strike Prices:

In a rising market, selling covered calls with higher strike prices provides additional room for the stock to appreciate before being called away. While the premiums for these calls are smaller, the trade-off is a higher potential profit if the stock rallies.

How it Works:

- Selling calls at a higher strike price will reduce the amount of premium you collect from the call, but it will allow the stock to run up higher before being called away. In a bull market, this additional capital appreciation will lead to greater returns.

Use Exploding Covered Calls

An exploding covered call is an advanced variation of the traditional covered call. This strategy combines selling a covered call with purchasing a long call at a higher strike price, allowing you to benefit from further upside even if your shares are called away. This technique is especially useful in bullish markets or when you expect a potential breakout in the underlying stock.

How it Works:

- **Sell a Call:** You sell a call option at a strike price where you're comfortable selling your shares. This generates premium income and caps your profit potential for the shares at the strike price if the stock is called away.

- **Buy a Call:** Simultaneously, you purchase a call option at a higher strike price, using a portion of the premium collected from the sold call to offset its cost. This long call provides the opportunity to profit from further price appreciation if the stock rallies beyond the sold call's strike price.

Advantages:

- **Premium Income:** Like a traditional covered call, you generate premium income if the equity remains below the strike price of the sold call at expiration.

- **Additional Upside Potential:** Unlike a traditional covered call, if the stock rises significantly, the value of the call you purchased will continue to rise, allowing you to sell it and capture the additional profit, turning what would have been a capped gain into an "exploding" opportunity.

Example:

Let's say you own 100 shares of a stock currently trading at $50, and you believe the stock may rally due to a major announcement. Here's how you can structure an exploding covered call:

- **Sell a Call:** Sell a $55 strike call for $2.00 per share, collecting $200 in premium.
- **Buy a Call:** Use part of this premium to buy a $65 strike call for $0.50 per share, costing $50 total.

Scenarios:

- **Stock Remains Below $55:** Both calls expire worthless. You keep your shares, and the net premium of $1.50 per share ($2.00 - $0.50), generating $150 in income. (along with any appreciation below $55)
- **Stock Rises to $70:** Your $55 strike call is exercised, but your $65 strike call adds extra profit:
    - **$5 per share** from selling the stock ($55 - $50).
    - **$1.50 per share** in net premium.
    - **$5 per share** from the $65 strike call ($70 - $65).
    - **Total Profit: $11.50 per share or $1,150.**

Key Considerations

Balance Premium and Risk: Using higher strike prices or exploding covered calls will reduce immediate premium income, in exchange for allowing you to capture more profit from the bullish momentum. Make sure the reduced income aligns with your broader strategy and cash flow needs if the bullish move doesn't pan out as expected.

Market Timing: These strategies are best used when you have a strong expectation of continued bullish momentum.

Costs and Expirations: Ensure the long call in an exploding covered call strategy is appropriately priced and aligned with the expiration of the short call to simplify risk management.

Navigating Bear Markets: Preserving Capital and Profiting in Downward Trends

Bear markets, characterized by falling stock prices and heightened volatility, present unique challenges for traders using The Wheel strategy. Without thoughtful adjustments, this strategy can expose you to significant downside risk, especially if you are assigned shares that continue to lose value. However, by tailoring your trades to bearish conditions, you can mitigate losses and even generate income despite the market's overall decline.

Adapting Cash-Secured Puts

In a bear market, cash-secured puts require extra caution. Selling puts too close to the stock's current price increases the likelihood of assignment at levels that could quickly become unfavorable. To reduce this risk, you can adjust your strike prices downward, creating a greater margin of safety. While the premium will be smaller, the reduced assignment risk helps protect your portfolio in a declining market.

Shorter expiration dates are another effective way to manage risk. In a volatile environment, shorter-term trades allow you to reassess conditions more frequently and adjust your strategy as needed. Additionally, bear markets tend to see increased implied volatility (IV), which means even shorter-term options can offer attractive premiums.

For more advanced traders, replacing cash-secured puts with bull put spreads is a powerful way to limit risk while still collecting premium. A bull put spread involves selling a put at your desired strike price and buying a lower strike put as protection. This setup caps your maximum loss and reduces the capital required for the trade. For example, instead of setting aside $40,000 to sell a $40 strike put, you could create a spread by purchasing a $30 strike put with some of the credit you brought in from the put you sold. This would reduce your total profit slightly but also cap your maximum loss at less than $1,000 if the stock drops below $40.

Adjusting Covered Calls

Covered calls also need to be adapted in bear markets. When stock prices are steadily declining, selling in-the-money (ITM) calls becomes an effective way to lock in premium and reduce your cost basis as the stock price continues to go down. By choosing a strike price below the current stock price, you collect a higher premium and increase the likelihood of the shares being called away. This approach can help you exit a losing position at a manageable level while generating income.

Another powerful strategy is to create a collar trade. This involves using the premium from selling a call to purchase a put at a lower strike price, effectively protecting the value of your shares from further declines. For example, if you own shares of a stock trading at $50, you could sell a $55 call for $2 and use that premium to buy a $45 put. If the stock price falls below $45, the protective put ensures your losses are capped. While a collar trade limits your upside potential, it still allows you to make money if the equity rallies and provides peace of mind during turbulent markets.

Focusing on Defensive Stocks

Bear markets often impact different sectors unevenly, with defensive industries like utilities, healthcare, and consumer staples proving more resilient. Stocks in these sectors are less volatile and tend to experience smaller declines compared to growth or tech stocks. By focusing your Wheel trades on defensive stocks during bear markets, you can reduce the likelihood of large losses while maintaining steady premium income.

Managing Risk with Diversification and Hedging

Diversification becomes even more critical in bear markets. Concentrating too many trades in a single stock or sector amplifies your risk, especially during a downturn. By spreading your trades across multiple industries and asset types, you can mitigate the impact of losses in any one area.

Hedging can also play an important role. Consider using index options, inverse ETFs, or even simple protective puts on broader market indices to offset losses in your portfolio. For example, buying a put option on the S&P 500 can provide a safety net if the overall market continues to decline.

CHAPTER 7

MASTERING TIME DECAY

HOW TO MAKE TIME WORK IN YOUR FAVOR

TIME DECAY, OR THETA, is one of the most crucial factors in options trading, especially for traders using The Wheel strategy. As time passes, the extrinsic value of an option, its "time value," gradually erodes. For options sellers, this erosion works in your favor, as the premium you collect loses value over time, increasing the likelihood of keeping the full premium when the option expires worthless, or allowing you to buy the option back to close out the trade for a partial profit.

In this chapter, we'll take an in-depth look at how time decay works, how it impacts different strike prices, and how you can use this knowledge to your advantage.

What Is Time Decay?

Time decay is the gradual reduction in the extrinsic value of an option as expiration approaches. This happens because the less time an option has before it expires, the less chance there is for the underlying stock to move in a way that makes the option profitable for the buyer.

For options sellers, this is a key source of profit. Every day that passes works in your favor, provided the stock price doesn't move dramatically against your position.

How Time Decay Affects Strike Prices

Time decay doesn't impact all options equally. Its effect varies based on the relationship between the option's strike price and the current price of the underlying stock. To fully understand this concept, it's helpful to break it down into three categories: At-the-Money (ATM), Out-of-the-Money (OTM), and In-the-Money (ITM) options.

At-the-Money (ATM) Options

ATM options are options where the strike price is closest to the current market price of the stock.

- **Highest Extrinsic Value**:
  ATM options carry the most extrinsic value because they are at the

tipping point where the stock price could easily move in or out of profitability for the buyer. This makes them the most sensitive to time decay.

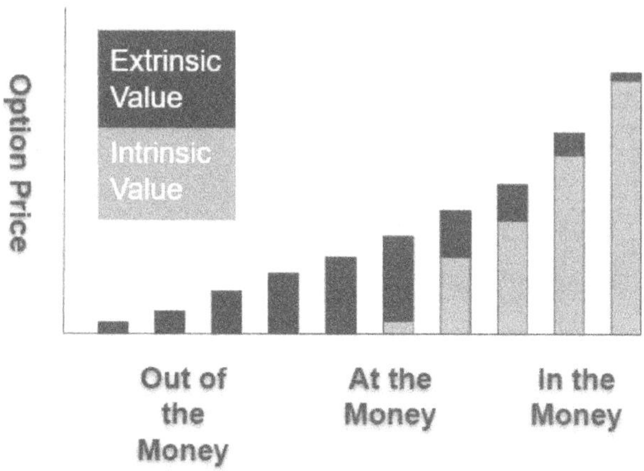

- **Fastest Time Decay:**
  As expiration approaches, ATM options lose their extrinsic value the fastest. This is why ATM options are particularly attractive to sellers in strategies like The Wheel—they provide the highest premiums up-front, but those premiums erode quickly.

- **Practical Example:**
  Suppose a stock is trading at $50, and you sell an ATM option with a $50 strike price for $2. The $2 premium consists entirely of extrinsic value. As expiration nears, this premium may rapidly decline to $0.10, even if the stock price doesn't move, allowing you to close the trade early or let it expire worthless.

Out-of-the-Money (OTM) Options

OTM options are options where the strike price is below the current stock price (for puts) or above the stock price (for calls).

- **Lower Extrinsic Value**:
  OTM options generally have less extrinsic value compared to ATM options because the likelihood of the option becoming profitable for the buyer is lower.

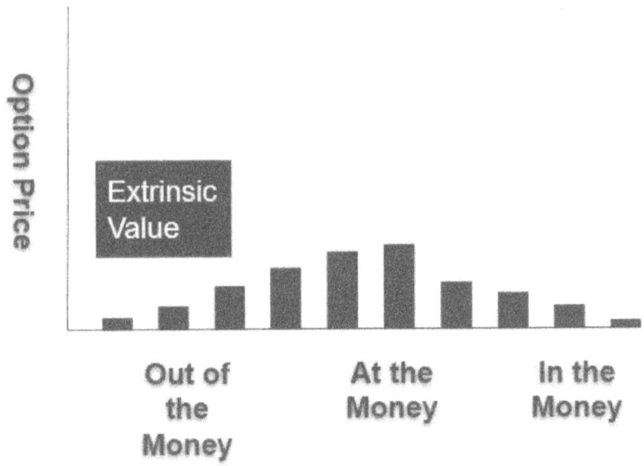

- **Slower Time Decay Initially**:
  OTM options lose value at a slower rate earlier in their life. However, as expiration nears and the chance of the stock reaching the strike price diminishes, the extrinsic value erodes rapidly.

- **Practical Example**:
  If a stock is trading at $50, and you sell an OTM put with a $45 strike price for $0.50, the premium may hold steady for weeks if the stock stays well above $45. As expiration nears, that premium may drop close to zero, particularly if the stock price remains far from the strike price.

In-the-Money (ITM) Options

ITM options are options where the strike price is above the current stock price (for puts) or below the stock price (for calls).

- **Value Dominated by Intrinsic Value**:

ITM options derive most of their value from intrinsic value (the difference between the stock price and the strike price). Their extrinsic value is lower than that of ATM options and decreases more gradually over time.

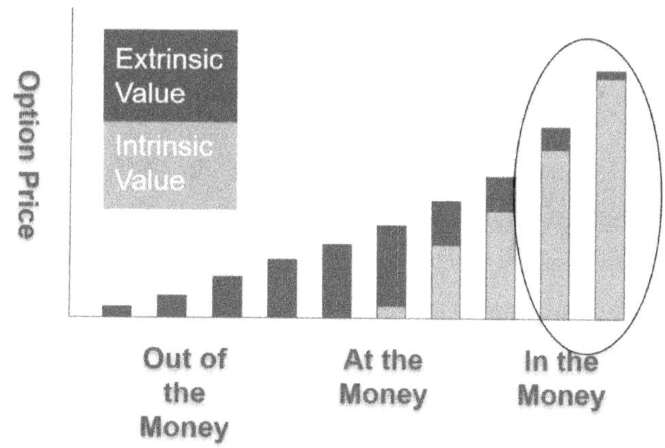

- **Less Affected by Time Decay:**
  Because extrinsic value is a smaller component of ITM options, time decay impacts them less than ATM or OTM options. Most of the value of an ITM option remains tied to the stock's movement, not the passage of time.

- **Practical Example:**
  If a stock is trading at $50, and you sell an ITM call with a $45 strike price for $7, the premium includes $5 of intrinsic value and $2 of extrinsic value. Over time, the $2 of extrinsic value will erode, but the $5 of intrinsic value will remain unless the stock price changes.

Understanding how time decay affects different strike prices can help you tailor your Wheel trades:

1. **Sell ATM Options** for the highest premiums and fastest decay, but be prepared for potential assignment.

2. **Sell OTM Options** for lower assignment risk and steadier decay, especially if you're focused on collecting premiums without acquiring shares.
3. **Sell ITM Options** for higher premiums when you're willing to own the stock or have shares called away at a profit.

Why Time Decay Accelerates Near Expiration

One of the most important concepts in options trading is that **theta decay is not linear**—it accelerates as expiration approaches. To understand why this happens, let's explore the mechanics behind time decay and how it relates to the perceived risk of the option for the buyer.

Early in the Option's Life: Slow Decay

When an option is written with a significant amount of time until expiration, its extrinsic value decays more slowly. During this period:

- **Plenty of Time for Price Movement**: The longer the time horizon, the higher the probability that the stock price could move significantly, either in favor of or against the option buyer.
- **Higher Extrinsic Value**: Because of this uncertainty, buyers are willing to pay more for the option, and extrinsic value decays gradually over time.

Think of this like renting a car for a month. The daily cost is lower because there's a long-term agreement in place, and both parties have time to adjust if something unexpected happens.

As Expiration Approaches: Accelerated Decay

In the final weeks or days leading up to expiration:

- **Narrowing Window for Movement**: With less time remaining, the probability of a significant price move decreases. For the option buyer, the likelihood of the option becoming profitable shrinks with each passing day.

- **Faster Decline in Extrinsic Value**: Because the "time cushion" is disappearing, the extrinsic value of the option erodes much more rapidly as expiration approaches.

Using the car rental analogy, think of this as renting a car for a single day. The cost per day is much higher because the agreement is short-term, and the flexibility to adapt is limited.

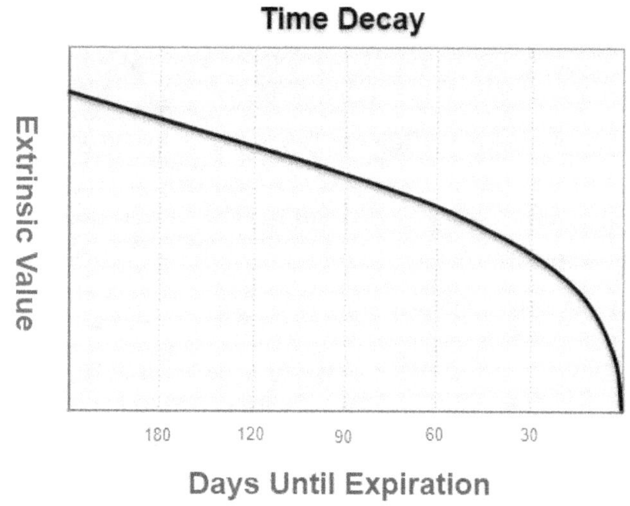

Why Selling Ultra-Short-Term Options Isn't Always Ideal

While the rapid time decay of short-term options may seem attractive, selling options that are too close to expiration can often be a mistake. Here's why:

- **Limited Extrinsic Value Remaining**:
  By the time an option is just a few days from expiration, much of the

extrinsic value has already eroded. This leaves little premium to collect, even though the seller is still taking on the full risk of the trade.

  - **Example:** If an option had $2 in extrinsic value 30 days before expiration, it might only have $0.10 left with two days remaining. Collecting this remaining premium may not justify the risk.

- **High Risk-to-Reward Ratio**:
  The small remaining premium often isn't worth the potential downside if the stock moves unexpectedly in the final hours before expiration.

- **Transaction Costs**:
  Frequent trading of ultra-short-term options can increase fees, further eroding potential profits.

The Sweet Spot for Selling Options

Most traders find that selling options with 2-6 weeks to expiration offers the best balance between collecting significant premium and benefiting from rapid time decay. This timeframe provides:

- Enough extrinsic value to make the trade worthwhile.
- The opportunity to capture the steepest part of the time decay curve without holding the trade too long.

By focusing on this "sweet spot," you can optimize your trades to maximize income while minimizing unnecessary risk.

How Price Action Impacts Time Decay

While time decay is a predictable and consistent factor in options trading, **price action**, the movement of the underlying stock, can significantly accelerate the erosion of an option's extrinsic value. This interplay between time decay and price movement creates opportunities for options sellers to capitalize on favorable conditions and manage their trades more effectively.

The Effect of Price Action on Puts

When you sell a cash-secured put, your goal is for the stock price to remain above the strike price until expiration, allowing the option to expire worthless. Price action can work in your favor well before expiration:

If the Stock Price Rises:

A sharp increase in the stock price reduces the likelihood of assignment, meaning the chance of the stock dropping below the strike price is now minimal. As a result:

- The extrinsic value of the put decreases rapidly because buyers are no longer willing to pay much for an option that is unlikely to become profitable.
- The put's premium drops, allowing you to potentially close the trade early for a profit.

Example: Closing a Cash-Secured Put Early

Suppose you sell a 30-day strike $45 cash-secured put for $2 when the stock is trading at $50. Your obligation is to potentially buy 100 shares of the stock at $45 if the stock price drops below the $45 strike price. You collect $2 per share, or $200 total, as premium when you enter the trade, dropping your cost basis down to $43 if you are assigned.

After one week, the stock price rises sharply to $55. With 23 days left until expiration, the market now views the $45 strike price as highly unlikely to be reached. The put option's premium drops significantly, falling to just $0.10.

At this point, you have two options:

1. Close the trade early by buying back the put option for $0.10 and free up your capital for a new opportunity.
2. Hold the trade for the remaining 23 days to potentially collect the remaining $0.10.

If you decide to close the trade early, here's how the profit is calculated:

- **Premium Received**: $2.00 per share ($200 for the contract).
- **Cost to Close**: $0.10 per share ($10 for the contract).
- **Net Profit**: $2.00 - $0.10 = $1.90 per share ($190 total).
- **Time Held**: 7 days out of the original 30-day contract.

To calculate your ROI for the trade, use the following formula:

$$ROI = \frac{Profit}{Capital\ at\ Risk} \times 100$$

Profit: $190

Capital at Risk: $4,300 ($45 strike price × 100 shares - $200 premium collected).

$$ROI = \frac{190}{4300} \times 100 = 4.42\%$$

ROI: You achieved a 4.42% ROI in just 7 days.

To understand the trade's efficiency over time, you can calculate the annualized ROI:

$$Annualized\ ROI = \frac{ROI}{Days\ Held} \times 365$$

ROI: 4.42%

Days Held: 7

$$Annualized\ ROI = \frac{4.42}{7} \times 365 = 230.47\%$$

Annualized ROI: 230.47%

This shows that up to this point, this has been a very efficient use of your trading capital.

Why Not Hold the Trade for the Remaining $0.10?

At first glance, holding the trade for the remaining $0.10 in premium may seem like a reasonable choice. After all, why leave money on the table? However, it's important to evaluate the risk-to-reward trade-off and overall capital efficiency of remaining in the trade.

The Real Risk-to-Reward Trade-Off

Ask yourself: Would you enter a new trade risking $4,300 to earn just $10?If not, why would you stay in a trade with these characteristics?

$$Risk\ to\ Reward\ Ratio = \frac{Maximum\ Risk}{Potential\ Reward}$$

- **Maximum Risk**: $4,300 (the capital required to fulfill the obligation to buy 100 shares at $45 if the stock drops unexpectedly).
- **Potential Reward**: $0.10 per share ($10 total).

$$Risk\ to\ Reward\ Ratio = \frac{4300}{10} = 430{:}\,1$$

- **Risk-to-Reward Ratio**: 430:1

ROI for Collecting the Remaining $0.10

$$ROI = \frac{Profit}{Capital\ at\ Risk} \times 100$$

- **Profit**: $0.10 × 100 = $10.
- **Capital at Risk**: $4,300.

$$ROI = \frac{10}{4300} \times 100 = 0.23\%$$

- **ROI**: 0.23%

Annualized ROI for the Remaining .10 Collected Over 23 Days

$$Annualized\ ROI = \frac{ROI}{Days\ Held} \times 365$$

- **ROI:** 0.23%
- **Days Held:** 7

$$Annualized\ ROI = \frac{0.23}{23} \times 365 = 3.65\%$$

- **Annualized ROI**: 3.65%

Holding out for the max profit yields an ROI of just 0.23% over 23 days, which annualizes to a mere 3.65%. Compared to the 230.47% annualized ROI achieved by closing early, holding the trade for minimal remaining premium is an inefficient use of capital.

The Better Decision: Use Your Capital Efficiently

By closing the trade early, you lock in $190 of profit and free up $4,300 in capital to deploy in new trades with better returns.

- You could use the capital to secure a new put with higher premium, generating additional income in less time.
- Repositioning your capital allows you to repeat trades with strong returns, compounding your gains more effectively.

Holding the trade for an additional $10 profit exposes you to unnecessary risk for minimal reward.

- Holding trades open until the options expire often yields poor ROI compared to closing early and redeploying capital.
- Always compare the risk-to-reward ratio of holding a trade versus opening a new one.
- Efficient capital allocation is the cornerstone of maximizing returns in The Wheel strategy.

Using the Greeks to Optimize Extrinsic Value

To fully master options trading and maximize your income from selling options, it's crucial to understand how **extrinsic value** interacts with the Greeks. While time decay (theta) plays a central role, other factors, such as delta and vega, also significantly influence extrinsic value. By considering these Greeks, you can make more informed decisions about which options to sell and when to adjust your trades.

Theta: Measuring the Erosion of Extrinsic Value

Theta, as previously discussed, represents the rate at which an option loses extrinsic value as time passes. For sellers, a higher theta means faster premium collection, but it also comes with trade-offs:

- **Options Closer to Expiration**:
  Options with fewer days to expiration typically have higher theta, meaning their extrinsic value erodes more quickly. However, they also have lower total premiums, so the potential reward may not always justify the associated risks.

- **Balancing Time and Premium**:
  Selling options with 2-6 weeks to expiration often strikes a good balance, capturing meaningful extrinsic value while benefiting from accelerating time decay as expiration nears.

Delta: Gauging the Probability of Assignment and Price Sensitivity

Delta serves two important roles for options sellers:

1. **Probability of Assignment**:
   Delta can be interpreted as the approximate likelihood that an option will finish in-the-money (ITM) at expiration. For instance:

   - A delta of 0.25 suggests a 25% chance the option will finish ITM and be assigned.

   - A lower delta (e.g., 0.1 to 0.2) indicates a lower probability of assignment, while a higher delta (e.g., 0.4 to 0.6) signals a greater likelihood of assignment.

2. **Price Sensitivity**:

Delta also represents the expected change in the option's price for every $1 move in the underlying stock. For example:

- If an option has a delta of 0.25, its price will increase or decrease by $0.25 per share ($25 per contract) for every $1 movement in the stock price.
- This sensitivity allows you to estimate how quickly the option's premium might decline with favorable price action, enabling you to calculate the likelihood of closing the trade early for partial profits.

Using Delta to Optimize Your Trades

- **Lower Delta (e.g., 0.1 to 0.2)**:These options provide lower premiums and a smaller likelihood of assignment. They are ideal if your primary goal is to collect premium without acquiring shares or losing them in the case of covered calls.
- **Moderate Delta (e.g., 0.2 to 0.3)**:Options in this range strike a good balance between premium collection and assignment probability. For The Wheel strategy, this range is often preferred, as it aligns with selling puts on stocks you're comfortable owning or selling calls on shares you're willing to part with.
- **Higher Delta (e.g., 0.4 to 0.6)**:These options have higher premiums and a greater likelihood of assignment, which can be beneficial if you want to acquire shares at a discount (puts) or liquidate shares you already own (calls).

Vega: Understanding the Impact of Implied Volatility (IV)

Vega measures the sensitivity of an option's price to changes in implied volatility (IV), which directly affects extrinsic value:

- **High IV Environments**:
  When IV is elevated, extrinsic value increases because the market expects larger price swings in the underlying stock.
  - **Benefit to Sellers**: Selling options during periods of high IV allows you to collect higher premiums.
  - **Trade-Off**: High IV can slow the impact of time decay, as the market prices in greater uncertainty.
- **Low IV Environments**:
  When IV is low, extrinsic value is reduced because the market expects smaller price movements.
  - **Impact on Time Decay**: Low IV accelerates the effect of theta, as there's less premium tied to market uncertainty.

Bringing It All Together: Using the Greeks to Evaluate Trades

The Greeks are powerful tools that help you assess and optimize your trades. By understanding how they interact, you can maximize extrinsic value, manage risk effectively, and refine your strategy to align with your goals. Here's how to apply them:

1. Choosing the Right Expiration (Theta)

Theta measures the rate at which an option loses value due to time decay. To capitalize on this, focus on options with an expiration that balances premium collection with risk management:

- **Short-Term Options (1-4 Weeks)**:These options offer rapid time decay, particularly as expiration nears. They are ideal for generating consistent income and allow you to adjust positions frequently.

- **Medium-Term Options (4-8 Weeks+)**:These options provide a good balance between premium collection and flexibility. While time decay isn't as fast early on, the higher premiums may justify the extended duration, especially if you expect delta or vega to reduce the extrinsic value faster.
- **Avoid Extremely Short-Term Options**:Options with just a few days to expiration often have minimal extrinsic value remaining. Selling these may not justify the risk, as most of the extrinsic value is already gone.

2. Selecting the Strike Price (Delta)

Delta serves as both a measure of probability and price sensitivity, helping you align trades with your goals:

- **Low Delta (0.10-0.20)**:Options with a low delta have a smaller likelihood of assignment, which translates to lower risk but also significantly smaller premiums. These are ideal for traders prioritizing income generation without the intent to acquire or sell shares. However, it's important to evaluate whether the return justifies the risk, as the lower premiums may not always make the trade worthwhile, especially after accounting for fees or potential margin requirements.
- **Moderate Delta (0.20-0.40)**:This range represents a balanced approach, offering a good mix of premium income and the probability of assignment. For The Wheel Strategy, this is often considered the sweet spot—selling puts on stocks you're comfortable owning at a discount or selling calls on shares you'd be happy to part with. Moderate delta options typically provide enough premium to make the trade appealing while keeping assignment risk manageable.
- **High Delta (0.40-0.60+)**:High-delta options have a greater likelihood of assignment, making them more suitable for traders with a

clear objective of acquiring shares (puts) or liquidating shares (calls). The higher premiums can be attractive, but the increased risk of assignment should align with your overall strategy. High-delta options can be particularly useful in trending markets where you anticipate favorable stock movement and want to capitalize on more aggressive positions.

3. Timing the Trade (Vega)

Vega reflects how implied volatility (IV) impacts an option's price, and understanding this can significantly improve your timing:

- **High IV Environments**:
  Elevated IV often signals higher extrinsic value, allowing you to collect larger premiums. However, be cautious—higher IV also reflects increased uncertainty and the possibility of significant price swings.
  - **Strategy Tip**: Consider selling options during periods of high IV to capitalize on elevated premiums but select strike prices that provide a comfortable margin of safety.
- **Low IV Environments**:
  Lower IV reduces extrinsic value and may limit your premium potential. However, the lower market uncertainty may align with conservative strategies.
  - **Strategy Tip**: In low-IV markets, focus on shorter expirations or strike prices with slightly higher deltas to maintain premium income.

Chapter 8

Dividend Risk and Opportunities

Exploring the Double-Edged Sword of Dividends

Dividend-paying stocks hold a unique appeal for investors seeking steady income and long-term growth. These stocks offer regular cash payouts, dividends, providing returns even when the stock price remains flat or experiences slight declines. Unlike growth stocks, which rely solely on price appreciation to generate returns, dividend stocks allow investors to realize tangible income without needing to sell shares.

Building a Portfolio for Passive Income

Investing in high-quality dividend-paying stocks can help create a reliable income stream, making them particularly attractive for certain types of investors:

- **Retirees**: Dividend income can supplement or replace traditional sources of retirement income, such as pensions or social security, providing financial stability.
- **Income-Focused Investors**: Individuals seeking consistent cash flow can rely on dividends to meet regular expenses or reinvest for future growth.
- **Wealth Builders**: Even for those in the accumulation phase, dividends provide an opportunity to grow wealth through reinvestment, enhancing returns over time.

For example, consider a stock that pays an annual dividend yield of 4%. By investing in a portfolio of similar stocks, an investor could generate $4,000 per year on a $100,000 investment, without selling a single share. Combined with the potential for stock price appreciation, the overall return can be substantial, especially when compounded over time.

The Power of Dividend Reinvestment (DRIP)

Many dividend investors opt to participate in a **Dividend Reinvestment Plan (DRIP)**, a program offered by most brokers and companies that automatically reinvests dividend payments into additional shares of the same stock. This strategy provides several key advantages:

- **Automatic Compounding**: By reinvesting dividends, investors effectively purchase more shares, which then generate additional dividends. Over time, this compounding effect accelerates portfolio growth, allowing even modest investments to grow significantly.
    - Example: If an investor receives $100 in dividends and reinvests it to purchase two more shares, those additional shares will generate their own dividends in subsequent cycles, creating a snowball effect.
- **Cost Averaging**: DRIP participants benefit from **dollar-cost averaging**, as dividends are reinvested regardless of the stock's current price. This helps smooth out the impact of market volatility, as shares are purchased at varying prices over time.
- **Hands-Off Growth**: DRIPs automate the reinvestment process, requiring no active management from the investor. This is particularly appealing for individuals focused on long-term wealth accumulation, as it eliminates the temptation to spend dividend income and ensures continuous growth.

Illustrating the Impact of DRIP

Consider an investor holding 100 shares of a dividend-paying stock priced at $50 per share, with an annual dividend yield of 4%. Without a DRIP, the investor would receive $200 in cash dividends annually. However, by reinvesting those dividends, the investor purchases four additional shares in the first year, increasing their share count to 104. The following year, those 104 shares generate dividends, which are again reinvested to buy even more shares.

Over 10 years, this compounding effect can result in significantly more shares and a much higher total portfolio value compared to simply taking the cash dividends.

Combining Dividends with The Wheel Strategy

For investors already focused on dividend-paying stocks, The Wheel strategy can serve as a powerful enhancement:

- **Cash-Secured Puts**: Selling puts allows you to acquire dividend stocks at a discount, reducing your cost basis. By purchasing shares at a lower price, your effective dividend yield increases, further boosting income.
- **Covered Calls**: Selling covered calls on dividend stocks adds a layer of income beyond the dividend itself. The premiums collected can be viewed as "bonus dividends," enhancing overall returns without requiring additional investments.

By integrating dividends with The Wheel strategy, investors can create a portfolio that maximizes both cash flow and long-term growth potential.

Dividend Risk: The Downside of Covered Calls

Covered calls on dividend-paying stocks can be a powerful strategy for generating additional income, but they come with a specific risk: **early assignment** by the option buyer seeking to capture the dividend payment. Understanding this risk is critical for managing your covered call positions effectively.

Understanding Early Assignment

Why Early Assignment Happens

Early assignment occurs when the buyer of your call option decides to exercise their right to purchase your shares before the expiration date, usually to capture the upcoming dividend. Here's the logic behind this decision:

1. **Retain the Option's Extrinsic Value**:

If the call option still has significant extrinsic value, the buyer is better off holding the option rather than exercising it. The extrinsic value represents the "time value" of the option, which they would forfeit by exercising early.

2. **Capture the Dividend**:
   If the dividend payment exceeds the remaining extrinsic value of the option, it may be financially advantageous for the buyer to exercise the option early. By doing so, they can own the stock before the ex-dividend date and receive the dividend.

Example:
Imagine a stock priced at $55 with a $50 strike call option that is ITM. If the dividend is $0.75 per share but the option's remaining extrinsic value is only $0.50, the buyer gains a net benefit of $0.25 per share by exercising early to capture the dividend.

Key Risk Factors for Early Assignment

1. **In-the-Money (ITM) Options**:
   Early assignment is almost always limited to ITM options—those where the stock price exceeds the strike price. This is because the buyer would not exercise an out-of-the-money (OTM) option, as they could purchase the stock for less than the strike price in the open market.

2. **Timing Around Ex-Dividend Dates**:
   The risk of early assignment spikes in the days leading up to the ex-dividend date, especially when the option is ITM and close to expiration. At this point:

   - **Time Decay**: The extrinsic value of the option may have eroded significantly.

   - **Dividend Incentive**: The dividend amount becomes a more prominent factor, increasing the likelihood of early assignment.

3. **Low Extrinsic Value**:
Early assignment is most likely when the remaining extrinsic value of the option is lower than the dividend payment. For example, if the dividend is $0.80 and the extrinsic value is $0.40, early assignment becomes a logical choice for the option buyer.

The Financial Logic of Early Assignment

Understanding the decision-making process for the buyer can help clarify the risk for the covered call seller:

- If the dividend exceeds the extrinsic value, the buyer may choose early assignment to "trade" the remaining time value for the guaranteed dividend.
- If the dividend is less than the extrinsic value, early assignment is unlikely because the buyer would lose more by forfeiting the time value than they would gain from the dividend.

How to Mitigate Dividend Risk

Managing dividend risk while benefiting from covered calls requires careful planning and adaptability. By adjusting your strategy based on the timing of ex-dividend dates, you can strike a balance between generating income and minimizing the risk of early assignment. Here are several strategies to consider:

1. Avoid Expirations Immediately After Ex-Dividend Dates

Options that expire right after an ex-dividend date are particularly vulnerable to early assignment because their extrinsic value tends to be minimal due to time decay. This makes it easier for the dividend payment to exceed the remaining option premium, incentivizing the buyer to exercise early.

- **Adjust Your Timing**:
  When selling covered calls on dividend-paying stocks, consider expiration dates that occur well before or after the ex-dividend date. This avoids the high-risk window when early assignment is most likely.

- **Strategic Example**:
  If the ex-dividend date is two weeks away, choose an expiration that occurs before the ex-dividend date or at least one week after. This ensures the option maintains enough extrinsic value to discourage early assignment.

2. Sell Covered Calls at Higher Strike Prices

Selling calls with higher strike prices reduces the likelihood of the option going in-the-money (ITM). Since early assignment is almost exclusively a risk for ITM options, selecting a higher strike price can significantly lower your exposure.

- **Aggressive vs. Conservative Approach**:
  - **When the Ex-Dividend Date is Not a Concern**:
    Use more aggressive strike prices closer to the stock's current price to maximize premiums and enhance returns.
  - **When Dividend Risk is Elevated**:
    Shift to higher strike prices, prioritizing the reduction of ITM risk over premium collection.

- **Example**:
  If a stock is trading at $50 with an upcoming dividend of $0.80, selling a $55 strike call rather than a $50 strike call decreases the likelihood of early assignment while still collecting a reasonable premium.

3. Monitor Extrinsic Value

As the ex-dividend date approaches, keep a close eye on the option's remaining extrinsic value. Early assignment becomes a significant risk when the dividend payment exceeds the extrinsic value.

- **Key Consideration**:
  If you notice the extrinsic value dropping below the expected dividend amount, it's time to consider buying back the option to prevent assignment.

- **Practical Example**:
  Suppose you sold a $50 strike call on a stock trading at $55, with a dividend of $0.90 per share. If the option's extrinsic value falls to $0.40, the risk of early assignment becomes high. Buying back the option for $0.40 locks in most of your premium and prevents losing the shares unexpectedly.

4. Focus on Stocks with Lower Dividend Yields

Stocks with lower dividend yields typically have smaller dividend payments, reducing the likelihood of early assignment.

- **When to Use This Approach**:
  If dividend risk is a concern, consider prioritizing stocks with lower yields. While the dividend payments may be smaller, they still enhance total returns when combined with premium income from covered calls.

- **Long-Term Consideration**:
  Stocks with consistently moderate yields often provide a better balance between income and reduced early assignment risk, especially for investors looking to execute The Wheel strategy repeatedly on the same

equities.

Adapt Your Strategy Based on Dividend Timing

Dividend-paying stocks can be an excellent addition to your portfolio, but the timing of ex-dividend dates should inform your approach if you intend to enhance your returns with Covered Calls:

- **When Dividend Risk is Low**:
    - Choose more aggressive strike prices to maximize premiums.
    - Select expiration dates that align closely with your overall strategy.
    - Focus on capturing as much premium as possible while managing risk.
- **When Dividend Risk is High**:
    - Opt for higher strike prices to reduce risk of the call going ITM.
    - Avoid expirations immediately after the ex-dividend date.
    - Monitor extrinsic value closely and be prepared to adjust or close positions early if needed.

Key Takeaways

- **Maximizing Rewards**: Dividend-paying stocks can create a powerful synergy with The Wheel strategy, generating multiple streams of income through dividends and option premiums.
- **Managing Risks**: Early assignment is a real concern but can be mitigated by strategically selecting expiration dates, strike prices, and monitoring extrinsic value.

- **Overall Benefit**: With careful planning, The Wheel strategy can enhance the returns of a dividend-focused portfolio while maintaining a strong income stream and minimizing risks.

Early assignment can happen at any time, not only on dividend stocks or near ex-dividend dates. Those factors simply increase the odds by providing financial incentive for the buyer to exercise their option early. You should always be prepared for the possibility of early assignment when you sell options.

CHAPTER 9

ADVANCED TECHNIQUES FOR EXPERIENCED TRADERS

STRATEGIES TO FINE-TUNE AND MAXIMIZE YOUR TRADES

AS YOU GAIN EXPERIENCE with The Wheel strategy, you'll discover opportunities to refine your approach and incorporate advanced techniques to enhance your returns. This chapter explores some outside-the-box strategies designed to help advanced traders looking to take their skills to the next level.

Partial Covered Calls: Balancing Income and Upside Potential

In the traditional Wheel strategy, you sell cash-secured puts to acquire shares and then sell covered calls on all assigned shares until they are called away. For example, if you sold five puts and were assigned 500 shares, you would typically sell five covered calls on those shares. This approach works well in stable or moderately bullish markets.

However, there are situations where selling covered calls on all your shares may not align with your goals. For instance, if you suspect the stock is on the verge of a strong rally, selling calls on all your shares could cap your profit potential, as any appreciation above the strike price of your calls would be forfeited. Alternatively, you may want to keep some of your shares as part of a longer-term investment strategy.

Partial covered calls offer a versatile solution, allowing you to tailor your approach based on your expectations and goals. By selling calls on only a portion of your shares, you can generate premium income while leaving the remaining shares uncapped to capitalize on significant upside. Additionally, partial covered calls can be used as part of a long-term growth strategy to gradually build up equity positions, enabling traders to balance income generation with portfolio growth.

Uncapping Your Upside

Partial covered calls are ideal in situations where you have reason to suspect a stock could rise aggressively but still want to generate income from your position while you wait. By selling calls on only a portion of your assigned shares, you can:

- **Generate Income**: Continue earning premium income from the calls sold, offsetting downside risks and boosting overall returns.
- **Preserve Upside Potential**: Profit from additional upside above the strike price of your call because some shares that remain uncapped, enabling you to profit fully from any sharp price increases.

This technique strikes a balance between securing income and leaving room for capitalizing on bullish momentum.

Example: Partial Covered Calls in Action

Let's say you've been assigned 300 shares of a stock at a cost basis of $45 per share through Step 1 of The Wheel strategy.

You have reason to believe the stock may rally due to an upcoming product launch, but you're also concerned that the hype surrounding the launch has already been priced into the stock's current value. To balance these conflicting expectations, you decide to sell only two covered calls (representing 200 shares) at a strike price of $50, collecting a premium of $1.50 per share ($300 total). You leave the remaining 100 shares uncapped, allowing them to benefit from any upside beyond $50 on those shares.

The new product is announced, and the stock price jumps to $55, and you decide to sell your remaining 100 shares at the higher price. Here's how your trade would play out:

For the 200 Shares Capped by the Calls:

- These shares are sold at the $50 strike price when the calls are exercised.
- Stock Appreciation per Share: $5 ($50 strike price - $45 cost basis).
- Option Premium: $1.50 per share.

- Total Profit: $1,300 [($5 stock appreciation + $1.50 premium) × 200 shares].

For the 100 Uncapped Shares:

- These shares are sold in the open market at the new price of $55.
- Stock Appreciation per Share: $10 ($55 market price - $45 cost basis).
- Total Profit: $1,000 ($10 × 100 shares).

To calculate your total profit in this trade, combine the profits from both the capped and uncapped shares:

- Capped Shares: **$1,300**.
- Uncapped Shares: **$1,000**.
- Total Profit: **$2,300**.

By using partial covered calls, you generated income from the premium on 200 shares while also profiting from the addition appreciation on the uncapped 100 shares. This strategic balance allowed you to capitalize on the stock's rally without sacrificing all potential upside.

Had the stock price stayed below $50, you would still have collected the premium from the two covered calls you sold ($300). You could then continue selling covered calls on the remaining shares until they are also called away, maintaining steady income from the position.

Partial Covered Calls to Build a Stock Portfolio

Anticipating a rally isn't the only reason to use partial covered calls. Advanced traders often use this technique to grow their long-term stock holdings over time.

The income generated from cash-secured puts and covered calls can accumulate over time, creating additional capital for reinvestment. With additional cash in hand, traders may choose to sell more cash-secured puts, increasing their position sizes. When assigned shares through these additional puts, traders can designate a portion of the newly acquired shares as part of their long-term portfolio. The remaining shares can then be liquidated using covered calls and the cash can be used to continue generating income.

Example of Portfolio Expansion

Suppose you originally set aside **$50,000** for trading The Wheel strategy. Over time, through consistent premium collection from selling cash-secured puts and covered calls, the accumulated profits grow this portion of your portfolio to **$75,000**.

At this point, you're faced with a decision: how to keep your growing capital actively working while maintaining appropriate risk management and diversification.

- **Option 1: Increasing Position Sizes**
  You could continue to scale up the number of cash-secured puts you sell to reflect your increased trading capital. However, this approach could lead to challenges with position sizing. Concentrating too much capital into a single equity or strategy increases risk, especially during market downturns or unexpected volatility.

- **Option 2: Building Long-Term Equity Positions**
  Alternatively, when assigned shares of a high-quality stock you're comfortable holding, you could choose to sell only enough covered calls to liquidate the original $50,000 of capital you had allocated for The Wheel strategy.

The remaining $25,000 worth of stock could then be held as a long-term equity position, to benefit from capital appreciation, dividends (if applicable), and the compounding effect of long-term investment.

Balancing Growth and Risk

By combining The Wheel strategy with long-term investment goals, you can:

1. **Continue Trading the Wheel**: The original $50,000 remains allocated for The Wheel, allowing you to maintain active income generation.
2. **Expand Your Portfolio**: The remaining $25,000 is invested in long-term equity positions, diversifying your overall portfolio and reducing reliance on a single strategy.
3. **Maintain Risk Management**: This approach ensures that you're not over-allocating funds to any one equity or exposing yourself to excessive risk through oversized positions.

Key Benefits of This Approach

- **Diversification**: Keeps a portion of your portfolio focused on long-term growth, separate from the active trading capital used for The Wheel strategy.
- **Compounding Returns**: Long-term investments benefit from potential stock appreciation, dividends, and reinvested earnings, accelerating overall portfolio growth.
- **Risk Control**: Prevents overexposure to short-term options strategies by capping the portion of your portfolio actively engaged in trading.

This hybrid approach allows you to make the most of your growing capital while maintaining a balanced and diversified portfolio.

Bull Put Spreads: A Capital-Efficient Alternative to Cash-Secured Puts

For traders looking to reduce capital requirements without relying on margin, bull put spreads provide an advanced yet effective alternative to traditional cash-secured puts. This strategy is particularly appealing for those prioritizing income generation over stock acquisition.

A bull put spread works by selling a put as the primary income-generating instrument and using a portion of the premium received to purchase a put at a lower strike price. This second put acts as a hedge, reducing the capital requirement and protecting against catastrophic losses in the event of a sharp market downturn. By capping potential losses, bull put spreads empower traders to manage risk more effectively while optimizing the use of their trading capital.

Some traders avoid bull put spreads because purchasing the long put reduces the maximum profit compared to selling naked or cash-secured puts. While this is true, the benefits of this strategy often far outweigh the drawbacks for traders who understand how to use options effectively. Even buying a deep out-of-the-money (OTM) long put, one that only slightly impacts your total profit, can significantly reduce the overall risk in the trade and offers a safety net against catastrophic losses.

Advantages of Bull Put Spreads

Flexible Risk Management:

Bull put spreads allow you to control the level of risk you're comfortable with.

- The closer the strike price of your long put is to the strike price of your short put, the lower your total risk in the trade. This makes the strategy more conservative, as the long put offers greater protection.

- On the other hand, the further the strike price of your long put is from your short put, the smaller the reduction in profit, making the trade more aggressive but with less downside protection.

This flexibility enables you to tailor the trade to match your market outlook and risk tolerance.

Reduced Collateral Requirements:

Unlike cash-secured puts, which require setting aside the full purchase price of the shares (strike price × 100 shares), a bull put spread significantly reduces the amount of capital required.

- With a bull put spread, the collateral requirement is only the difference between the strike prices of the short and long puts minus the premium received.
- This makes bull put spreads a more efficient use of capital, particularly for traders with smaller accounts or those who want to diversify across multiple trades.

Capped Maximum Loss:

One of the most significant advantages of bull put spreads is the long put's ability to cap losses.

- If the stock price plummets unexpectedly, the long put provides protection, limiting your loss to the difference between the strike prices minus the premium received.
- This defined-risk feature is especially valuable in volatile markets,

where sharp and unpredictable downturns can otherwise lead to devastating losses in traditional cash-secured puts.

Reduced Margin Requirement:

Unlike selling naked puts on margin, bull put spreads can reduce your risk without requiring the use of margin and exposing you to the risk of margin calls.

- With naked puts on margin, a significant drop in the stock price can trigger a margin call, forcing you to either deposit additional funds or liquidate positions at unfavorable prices.
- Bull put spreads eliminate this risk entirely because your potential loss is predetermined and fully covered by the collateral requirement.

Example: Structuring an Ultra-Wide Bull Put Spread

Imagine you've selected a stock to use for The Wheel strategy. The equity is currently trading at $395, and you're evaluating two approaches: a traditional Wheel, where you start with a cash-secured put, and an Advanced Wheel, where you use an ultra-wide bull put spread. Both trades use options with 30 days until expiration. Let's break them down:

Cash-Secured Put

Sell a strike $340 Put and collect $11.05 per share of premium:

- You receive **$11.05 per share**, or **$1,105 per contract** (since each contract represents 100 shares).
- Since this is a cash-secured put, you must set aside the total amount required to purchase the stock at the strike price minus the premium received:

- **Return on Risk (ROR)**:

$$ROR = \frac{Premium\ Collected}{Risk\ Capital} = \frac{\$1{,}105}{\$32{,}895} = 3.36\%$$

- **Annualized ROR**:

$$Annualized\ ROR = \frac{ROR}{Days\ in\ the\ Trade} \times 365 = \frac{3.36}{30} \times 365 = 40.88\%$$

While an annualized return of 40.88% is impressive, let's see if we can achieve even better capital efficiency and risk management by using an ultra-wide bull put spread instead.

Ultra-Wide Bull Put Spread

Sell a Strike $340 Put for $11.05 and **Buy a Strike $200 Put for $0.39**:

- Selling the $340 put generates $11.05 per share in credit, while buying the $200 put costs $0.39 per share in debit. The net premium is calculated as:

$$Net\ Premium = Credit\ from\ Short\ Put - Debit\ from\ Long\ Put$$

$$Net\ Premium = 11.05 - 0.39 = \$10.66\ per\ share, or\ \$1{,}066\ per\ contract$$

- A bull put spread caps your potential loss at the difference between the strike prices of the puts, minus the net premium:

$$Risk\ Capital = (Difference\ Between\ Strikes - Net\ Premium) \times 100$$

$$Risk\ Capital = (\$340 - \$200 - \$10.66) \times 100 = \$129.34 \times 100 = \$12{,}934$$

- **Return on Risk (ROR)**: The ROR reflects the return based on the amount of capital at risk.

$$ROR = \frac{Net\ Premium}{Risk\ Capital} = \frac{\$1{,}066}{\$12{,}934} = 8.24\%$$

- **Annualized ROR**:

$$Annualized\ ROR = \frac{ROR}{Days\ in\ Trade} \times 365 = \frac{8.24}{30} \times 365 = 100.25\%$$

Analysis

1. Reduced Risk Capital:
The bull put spread reduces the collateral requirement by **$19,961**, allowing you to free up significant capital for other trades or investments.

2. Higher Efficiency:
The bull put spread delivers more than **double the ROR** compared to the cash-secured put while still offering a competitive maximum profit.

3. Risk Management:
The addition of the long put caps your maximum potential loss, protecting you from catastrophic losses if the stock price drops sharply.

Why Choose an Ultra-Wide Bull Put Spread?

- **Income-Focused Trading:** This approach works best for traders who prioritize generating income rather than acquiring shares.
- **Capital Efficiency:** The significantly lower collateral requirement allows you to trade more contracts, diversify your positions, or simply keep more cash available.
- **Defined Risk:** Unlike selling naked puts or cash-secured puts, the risk is capped, making this strategy suitable for volatile markets or cautious traders.

By using this advanced approach, you gain flexibility, maximize your capital efficiency, and achieve superior returns on risk compared to the traditional Wheel strategy.

Key Considerations for Bull Put Spreads

1. **Assignment Risk:**
   Even though the bull put spread is designed to limit risk, the short put can still result in assignment if the stock price falls below the strike price. However, the long put acts as a safety net, offsetting losses beyond its strike price and capping your maximum risk.

It's important to remember that this strategy is typically **not about acquiring shares**, unlike the traditional Wheel strategy. Instead, the focus is on **income generation** through collecting premiums. For traders seeking to avoid assignment entirely, monitoring the stock price and proactively managing the trade before expiration is essential.

- **Pro Tip:** Keep an eye on the relationship between the stock price and the strike prices. If the stock approaches the short put's strike, you might consider closing the trade early to avoid assignment or rolling the position to a later expiration date.

While the profit potential is reduced, the improved **risk-to-reward ratio** often makes this strategy worthwhile for traders focused on maximizing returns relative to risk capital.

- **Example:** In the earlier scenario, the bull put spread reduced the collateral requirement by nearly $20,000 while still delivering over **100% annualized ROR**, a stark improvement compared to the cash-secured put.

Rolling Strategies: Adjusting to Unexpected Moves

In an ideal scenario, the stock's price stays within your expected range, allowing your options to expire worthless or be assigned at your preferred strike price. However, markets are unpredictable, and stocks don't always move as expected. When this happens, rolling provides a powerful tool to adapt your strategy by adjusting the strike price, expiration date, or both. Rolling can help you manage risk, defer assignment, and optimize profits, but it's important to execute this adjustment correctly to maximize its effectiveness.

Key to Successful Rolling: Timing is Crucial

One of the most critical aspects of rolling is **when** you decide to adjust the trade. Waiting too long, especially until the option is deeply **in-the-money (ITM)** or near expiration, can significantly increase the cost of rolling. This is because rolling ITM options involves paying for both the intrinsic and extrinsic value of the current option.

- **Roll Early When the Option is Still Out-of-the-Money (OTM):** Adjusting the position while the option is still OTM keeps the cost lower since there's no intrinsic value to account for. The trade can still be adjusted at a reasonable cost, preserving the overall profitability of your strategy.

- **Why Early Adjustments Matter:**
  Rolling an OTM option allows you to reset the trade with less capital outlay while taking advantage of favorable market conditions. Delaying until the option is ITM forces you to cover the intrinsic value, which may make rolling cost-prohibitive or negate the potential benefits.

Types of Rolling Strategies

1. Rolling Down and Out (Puts):

When a stock's price falls sharply, the likelihood of assignment increases, and the short put's premium balloons as its intrinsic value grows. By rolling the put to a **lower strike price** and a **later expiration**, you can:

- **Reduce Your Cost Basis:** Adjusting the strike price downward lowers the price at which you agree to buy the stock, reducing the potential loss on assignment.
- **Defer Assignment:** Extending the expiration date buys you time for the stock price to recover while allowing the new put to collect premium through time decay.

2. Rolling Up and Out (Calls):

When a stock's price rises significantly, your short call may move **in-the-money (ITM)**, capping your upside. By rolling the call to a **higher strike price** and a **later expiration**, you can:

- **Capture More Upside Potential:** The higher strike price increases the amount you can sell the stock for if assigned, while the additional premium reduces your effective cost basis further.
- **Extend the Trade:** A later expiration gives you more time to collect premium while maintaining exposure to further price increases.

Key Considerations for Rolling

Assignment Risk:

- Even with rolling, assignment remains a possibility, especially with ITM options. Rolling down and out defers assignment but doesn't eliminate it, so always assess whether this aligns with your strategy.

Costs vs. Benefits:

- Rolling involves closing the original option and opening a new one. Ensure that the cost of closing the current position doesn't outweigh the potential benefits of the new trade.

- Analyze the impact of additional transaction fees and the bid-ask spread when rolling.

Timing:

- Rolling early keeps costs low, as it avoids paying for intrinsic value in ITM options.
- Monitor the **delta** and **vega** of the option, as these Greeks will influence the cost and potential outcomes of rolling.

Market Conditions:

- Evaluate broader market trends and implied volatility levels before rolling. If you expect the equity will continue moving in a way that would cause the trade to break again after it has been rolled, consider closing the trade entirely or adjusting to a new trade that benefits from the expected trend.

By understanding the importance of timing and how to effectively manage the interplay of strike prices and expiration dates, you can use rolling strategies to adapt to unexpected market moves while staying aligned with your financial goals.

Customizing Expirations: Enhancing Flexibility in The Wheel Strategy

It's easy to fall into the habit of using the same expiration cycle repeatedly, whether it's weekly, biweekly, or monthly options. For many traders, this approach works well for the majority of trades, offering consistency and simplicity.

However, advanced traders can unlock greater potential by tailoring expiration dates to specific market conditions or strategic goals.

Why Customize Expirations?

Customizing expiration dates gives traders the ability to adapt their strategy to specific market conditions and events. Advanced traders can fine-tune their approach to optimize premium collection, mitigate risks, and align with critical market events.

Align with Market Events

Significant market events, like earnings announcements, ex-dividend dates, Federal Reserve decisions, or major economic reports such as job data, can create unique opportunities and risks. Adjusting your typical trading patterns to account for these events can enhance returns or reduce the likelihood of adverse outcomes.

1. Trading Around Ex-Dividend Dates
For traders selling covered calls on dividend-paying stocks:

- **Adjusted Pattern:** When an ex-dividend date is approaching, consider selling a longer-term call (e.g., monthly) at a higher strike price. This reduces the likelihood of early assignment by ensuring the call retains enough extrinsic value to disincentivize the buyer from exercising early to capture the dividend.
- **Why This Works:** Longer expirations provide higher extrinsic value, which reduces early assignment risk, while a higher strike price leaves room for additional upside if the stock rallies.

2. Adjusting for Earnings Announcements
Earnings reports are often accompanied by heightened implied volatility (IV), which inflates option premiums, and a subsequent IV crush after the event.

- **Avoiding Assignment Risk:** If you typically sell puts two weeks out, consider extending the expiration by a week or two and selecting a lower strike price. This reduces the chance of assignment if the stock moves unpredictably after the earnings report.

- **Capitalizing on Elevated IV:** If you're okay with being assigned shares, sell at-the-money (ATM) puts that expire shortly after the earnings announcement. This allows you to collect higher premiums before the report and take advantage of the rapid IV reduction post-earnings.

3. Navigating Macroeconomic Events
Major economic data releases, such as non-farm payroll reports, GDP updates, or Federal Reserve rate decisions, often lead to market-wide volatility.

- **Adjusted Pattern:** For puts, consider selling options expiring after the event with a lower strike price to reduce risk during potential market turbulence. For covered calls, aim for expirations that bypass the event entirely if you expect the market to rally on good news.

- **Why This Works:** By shifting expiration dates to avoid high-volatility windows, you can protect your positions from unpredictable swings while still benefiting from time decay.

Maximize Time Decay

Time decay is a core element of options trading, and customizing expirations lets you strategically target periods when decay is most beneficial.

- **Short-Term Expirations:** If you expect minimal price movement and want to capture premium quickly, shorter expirations (1-2 weeks) are ideal.

- **Extended Expirations:** If the market is volatile, longer expirations can provide more stability and larger premiums, while still benefiting from time decay over the duration of the trade.

Adjust for Implied Volatility (IV)

Implied volatility fluctuates based on upcoming events and market conditions, and expiration dates play a significant role in how traders can capitalize on or protect against these changes.

- **Leveraging High IV:** When IV is elevated (e.g., before earnings or major events), selling options with slightly longer expirations can capture inflated premiums.
- **Avoiding Low IV:** When IV is low, shorter expirations may be more effective, as options premiums will already be compressed, and time decay can provide faster returns.

Different events require different strategies. Customizing expirations allows traders to add precision to their strategies, ensuring they are positioned for success no matter the market conditions.

Key Takeaways: Unlocking Advanced Techniques for The Wheel Strategy

The advanced techniques explored in this chapter allow traders to elevate their execution of The Wheel strategy, tailoring it to meet specific goals and adapt to changing market conditions. Here's a summary of the key concepts:

Partial Covered Calls: Combining Income and Upside Potential

- **Core Advantage:** Generate premium income from covered calls while leaving a portion of shares uncapped to benefit from potential rallies.

- **When to Use:** Ideal in bullish markets or when you expect a stock to experience a significant upside, allowing you to capitalize on growth while still securing income.
- **Long-Term Benefits:** Useful for portfolio expansion, enabling traders to strategically hold long-term equity positions while maintaining a steady income stream.

Bull Put Spreads: Reducing Collateral Requirements and Limiting Risk

- **Core Advantage:** Replace traditional cash-secured puts with a bull put spread to reduce the capital required to secure the trade and cap potential losses.
- **When to Use:** Best suited for traders focused on income generation rather than stock acquisition or for those with limited capital who want to optimize their risk-to-reward ratio.
- **Strategic Insight:** Enables advanced traders to free up capital for other trades while maintaining defined risk parameters, avoiding the need for margin or large collateral.

Rolling Strategies: Adapting to Unexpected Market Movements

- **Core Advantage:** Provides flexibility to adjust strike prices and expiration dates to respond to sudden stock price movements.
- **When to Use:** Useful when a trade is not progressing as planned—whether the stock is rising or falling—to avoid assignment or capture additional upside.
- **Key Insight:** Rolling early, while the option is still out-of-the-money

(OTM), helps minimize costs and retain control over your portfolio.

Custom Expirations: Targeting Specific Time Frames and Events

- **Core Advantage:** Align expiration dates with key market events, like earnings announcements or ex-dividend dates, to optimize premium collection and manage risks.
- **When to Use:** For stocks with high implied volatility or during periods of significant market activity, choosing customized expiration dates can enhance returns or reduce assignment risk.
- **Strategic Flexibility:** Experimenting with shorter or longer expirations allows traders to adapt their strategy based on market conditions and personal goals.

Maximizing Opportunities with Advanced Techniques

Incorporating these advanced strategies into The Wheel not only enhances profitability but also increases flexibility and control. While the traditional Wheel strategy provides a solid foundation, these refinements allow experienced traders to:

- Unlock new income streams while managing risk.
- Adapt to volatile markets with confidence.
- Optimize capital efficiency to make the most of their portfolio.

By mastering these advanced techniques, you can turn The Wheel strategy into a powerful, versatile tool that evolves with your trading journey.

CHAPTER 10

LONG-TERM WEALTH ACCUMULATION

BUILDING A LEGACY WITH THE WHEEL STRATEGY

THE WHEEL STRATEGY ISN'T just a tool for generating short-term income—it can play a vital role in building long-term wealth. By reinvesting premiums, blending strategies, and diversifying across multiple equities, traders can create a robust portfolio designed to grow steadily over time. Let's explore how to align The Wheel with broader wealth-building goals.

Compounding Growth: The Power of Reinvestment

One of the simplest yet most effective ways to build wealth is through the power of compounding. By reinvesting the premiums earned from selling options, traders can accelerate portfolio growth.

- **Reinvesting Premiums:**
  Use the premiums collected from puts and calls to buy additional shares of stocks you believe in for the long term. Over time, these reinvestments increase the number of shares you own, which in turn increases your income potential from dividends and future covered calls.

- **Funding New Trades:**
  Alternatively, you can use premiums to fund additional Wheel trades. For example, if you've collected $1,000 in premiums, you can use that to secure another cash-secured put, creating a self-reinforcing cycle of income generation and portfolio expansion.

Blending Strategies: Combining The Wheel with Other Approaches

The Wheel is versatile and pairs well with other long-term strategies, enabling traders to tailor their approach to their financial goals and risk tolerance.

- **Dividend Reinvestment Plans (DRIPs):**
  For dividend-paying stocks, you can combine The Wheel with a DRIP to reinvest dividends and grow your share count automatically. The premiums from puts and calls act as an additional "dividend," compounding your returns even further.

- **Sector Rotation:**
  Incorporate The Wheel into a sector rotation strategy by targeting industries with favorable conditions. For example, during a technology boom, focus your Wheel trades on tech ETFs or stocks, then rotate into defensive sectors during economic downturns.

- **Growth-Oriented Stocks:**
  While The Wheel is often associated with stable, income-generating stocks, you can adapt it to higher-growth equities. By setting strike prices conservatively, you can capture premiums without being overly exposed to the volatility of growth stocks.

Portfolio Diversification: Spreading Risk for Stability

Diversification is a cornerstone of any wealth-building strategy, and The Wheel is no exception. By applying the strategy across multiple equities or ETFs, you can reduce the impact of a single stock's poor performance.

- **Across Multiple Equities:**
  Avoid concentrating your trades in one or two stocks. Instead, spread your Wheel trades across different companies and sectors. For example, you might sell puts on a tech stock, a consumer staples company, and a healthcare ETF to balance risk.

- **Using ETFs for Diversification:**
  ETFs can be an excellent choice for The Wheel, as they inherently provide exposure to a broad range of assets. Selling options on ETFs like SPY (S&P 500) or QQQ (Nasdaq-100) offers the benefits of diversification while maintaining the income potential of The Wheel.

- **Example of Diversification in Action:**
  A trader with a $100,000 portfolio might allocate $30,000 to sell puts on individual stocks, $40,000 to sell puts on ETFs, and keep $30,000 in cash reserves for flexibility. This balanced approach minimizes risk

while maximizing income potential.

The Role of Time: Staying Committed to the Process

Long-term wealth accumulation requires patience and discipline. The Wheel strategy is most effective when applied consistently over years, allowing the compounding effects of premiums, dividends, and stock appreciation to take hold.

- **Managing Risk Over Time:**
  Adjust strike prices and expiration dates to adapt to market conditions, but remain committed to reinvesting profits and diversifying your portfolio.
- **Tracking Progress:**
  Regularly review your portfolio to ensure it aligns with your long-term goals. Consider using a spreadsheet or portfolio tracker to monitor income, reinvestments, and growth over time.

Conclusion

Turning Knowledge into Results

Throughout this book, we've explored the ins and outs of The Wheel strategy, a powerful approach to generating income and building wealth through options trading. From the foundational steps to advanced techniques, you now have a comprehensive understanding of how to leverage The Wheel in different market conditions, manage risks effectively, and tailor the strategy to suit your financial goals.

The Wheel strategy is more than just a method for short-term income—it's a versatile framework for long-term wealth building. By consistently applying its principles, you can create multiple streams of income, compound your returns, and maintain control over your financial journey. Whether you're using cash-secured puts to acquire shares at a discount, covered calls to enhance income, or advanced techniques to maximize efficiency, The Wheel strategy offers opportunities for traders of all experience levels.

Key Takeaways

1. **Simplicity with Flexibility:** The Wheel's core principles are straightforward, but its applications are diverse. With a clear understanding of its mechanics, you can adapt the strategy to align with your risk tolerance and market outlook.

2. **The Power of Compounding:** Reinvesting premiums and dividends can accelerate portfolio growth over time, turning modest returns into significant wealth through the magic of compounding.

3. **Risk Management is Paramount:** Success in options trading isn't just about maximizing profits; it's about minimizing losses. From selecting the right strike prices to rolling positions strategically, every decision should be made with risk management in mind.

4. **Advanced Techniques for Growth:** Partial covered calls, bull put spreads, and customized expirations open new doors for experienced traders, enabling you to refine your approach and achieve greater returns with less capital at risk.

Turning Knowledge Into Skills

At this point, you've gained a deep understanding of The Wheel strategy, but knowledge alone isn't enough. Knowledge, without action, is trivia. The true value of this book lies in your ability to transform these concepts into skills. The difference between a trader who merely knows and one who succeeds is action. To reap the rewards of The Wheel strategy, you must take what you've learned and apply it consistently in the real world.

Start small, take calculated risks, and learn from each trade you make. Experiment, adapt, and refine your approach as you grow. Every successful trader was once where you are now—armed with knowledge and ready to take the first step. The only way to master The Wheel strategy is to use it.

Looking Forward

The financial markets are always evolving, and so too are the opportunities within them. As you continue your trading journey, remember that education and adaptability are your greatest assets. Keep refining your skills, stay informed about market trends, and never stop learning. The strategies you've mastered in this book are a solid foundation, but the best traders know that growth comes from continuous improvement.

A Final Word of Encouragement

Options trading, like any worthwhile endeavor, requires patience, discipline, and a willingness to learn from both successes and mistakes. The Wheel strategy is a tool, and how you use it will ultimately determine your outcomes. Approach each trade with curiosity and care, and don't be afraid to experiment and adjust as you gain experience.

This book is not the end of your journey but the beginning of a new chapter. Whether you're trading for income, building a legacy, or pursuing financial independence, The Wheel strategy can help you achieve your goals. Now it's your turn to take the concepts you've learned and put them into action.

Your financial future is in your hands. Turn the wheel, and let the opportunities roll.

References

Agarwal, V., & Naik, N. Y. (2004). Risks and portfolio decisions involving options. The Journal of Finance, 59(6), 2817–2846. https://doi.org/10.1111/j.1540-6261.2004.00714.x

Black, F., & Scholes, M. (1973). The pricing of options and corporate liabilities. Journal of Political Economy, 81(3), 637–654. https://doi.org/10.1086/260062

Chicago Board Options Exchange. (n.d.). Educational resources. Retrieved from https://www.cboe.com

Chicago Board Options Exchange (CBOE). (n.d.). Understanding options trading. Retrieved from https://www.cboe.com/

CBOE Options Institute. (n.d.). Options strategies: A guide for investors. Chicago Board Options Exchange. Retrieved from https://www.cboe.com

CBOE Options Institute. (n.d.). Options trading strategies. Chicago Board Options Exchange. Retrieved from https://www.cboe.com

CBOE Options Institute. (n.d.). Understanding advanced options strategies. Retrieved from https://www.cboe.com

Damodaran, A. (1996). Corporate finance: Theory and practice. Wiley.

Damodaran, A. (2012). Investment valuation: Tools and techniques for determining the value of any asset (3rd ed.). Wiley.

Dividend.com. (n.d.). Dividend investing strategies and insights. Retrieved from https://www.dividend.com

Fabozzi, F. J., & Drake, P. P. (2010). The basics of finance: An introduction to financial markets, business finance, and portfolio management. Wiley.

Fabozzi, F. J., & Grant, J. L. (2004). Handbook of financial engineering. McGraw-Hill.

Fabozzi, F. J. (2014). Handbook of fixed-income securities (8th ed.). McGraw-Hill Education.

Fidelity Investments. (n.d.). Advanced options strategies and portfolio applications. Retrieved from https://www.fidelity.com

Fidelity Investments. (n.d.). Dividend reinvestment and strategies for long-term growth. Retrieved from https://www.fidelity.com

Graham, B., & Dodd, D. (2008). Security analysis: Principles and techniques (6th ed.). McGraw-Hill Education.

Hull, J. C. (2018). Options, futures, and other derivatives (10th ed.). Pearson.

Internal Revenue Service. (2023). Publication 550: Investment income and expenses (including capital gains and losses). Retrieved from https://www.irs.gov

Investopedia. (n.d.). Capital gains tax: What it is and how it works. Retrieved from https://www.investopedia.com

Investopedia. (n.d.). Dividend reinvestment plans (DRIPs). Retrieved from https://www.investopedia.com

Investopedia. (n.d.). Options trading: A beginner's guide. Retrieved from https://www.investopedia.com/

Investopedia. (n.d.). Options trading basics and strategies. Retrieved from https://www.investopedia.com

Investopedia. (n.d.). Options trading strategies. Retrieved from https://www.investopedia.com

Investopedia. (n.d.). Options trading strategies for advanced traders. Retrieved from https://www.investopedia.com

Investopedia. (n.d.). Wash-sale rule. Retrieved from https://www.investopedia.com

Katsanos, A. (2010). Trading systems and methods (5th ed.). Wiley.

McMillan, L. G. (2012). Options as a strategic investment (5th ed.). New York Institute of Finance.

Morningstar. (n.d.). Dividend investing resources. Retrieved from https://www.morningstar.com

Natenberg, S. (1994). Option volatility and pricing: Advanced trading strategies and techniques. McGraw-Hill Education.

Options Clearing Corporation. (n.d.). Margin and risk management tools. Retrieved from https://www.theocc.com

Options Industry Council (OIC). (n.d.). Advanced options strategies guide. Retrieved from https://www.optionseducation.org

Schwab Center for Financial Research. (2023). Tax-efficient investing strategies. Retrieved from https://www.schwab.com

Schwab, C. (n.d.). Strategies for experienced options traders. Retrieved from https://www.schwab.com

Schwab, C. (n.d.). Understanding dividends and reinvestment strategies. Retrieved from https://www.schwab.com

Shreve, S. E. (2004). Stochastic calculus for finance I: The binomial asset pricing model. Springer.

Siegel, J. J. (2014). Stocks for the long run: The definitive guide to financial market returns and long-term investment strategies (5th ed.). McGraw-Hill Education.

Sincere, M. (2014). Understanding options (2nd ed.). McGraw-Hill Education.

Tastytrade. (n.d.). Educational content on options trading and risk management. Retrieved from https://www.tastytrade.com

Thales of Miletus. (n.d.). Early financial speculation in olive presses. Retrieved from historical archives.

Wiley, J., & Sons. (n.d.). The complete guide to option pricing formulas. Retrieved from https://www.wiley.com

Zacks Investment Research. (n.d.). Understanding options trading. Retrieved from https://www.zacks.com

Zacks Investment Research. (n.d.). Understanding tax implications for options trading. Retrieved from https://www.zacks.com

THREE SIMPLE
OPTION
STRATEGIES
TO GENERATE
INCOME
HOW TO REPLACE FULL-TIME INCOME
SELLING CREDIT SPREADS PART-TIME
SCHOLARLY MIND CREATIONS, LLC

CONTENTS

Introduction

Navigating Options Markets

When most people think about investing, they typically focus on buying stocks, following the mantra: buy low, sell high. With stock investments, you only make money when the market is rising. However, this isn't the only way to generate profits in the stock market. Instead of trading stocks, we will explore trading options.

The concept of options isn't new; it dates back to Ancient Greece, but modern options have only been around for a few decades. With options, instead of directly buying or selling shares, you purchase or sell contracts that give you the right to take specific actions, such as buying or selling shares of stock at a future date.

In the upcoming chapters, we will uncover the powerful ways these contracts can be used to generate cash flow. By the time you finish this book, you will be equipped with proven strategies that allow you to profit, regardless of market direction, whether it rises, falls, or remains steady.

One of the great things about options trading is that you don't need much money to get started. Unlike buying stocks, which often require a significant investment, options allow you to control shares with a relatively small amount of cash. This makes it easier for beginners to start trading without risking too much. No one likes to lose money, but you can keep your risks manageable with options. As you become more comfortable, you can gradually increase your trading capital as you see fit.

As your portfolio grows, trading can become even more exciting. With more capital, you can explore additional strategies and seize more opportunities. If you aim for a specific monthly income, having more money to trade with will enable you to make safer trades while still reaching your target, reducing your overall risk. However, when starting, it's perfectly fine to begin small and build your way up as you learn.

This book has a clear and powerful objective: to simplify complex concepts, making them easily understandable for everyone, regardless of their background or experience. With more than a decade of experience teaching online classes and providing 1-on-1 tutoring, I have successfully guided new investors to become confident traders and helped seasoned traders sharpen their strategies, leading to improved results and reduced risk. I understand that not everyone has the time or flexibility to attend live classes or the means for one-on-one tutoring, which is why I took the initiative to write this book. My goal is to ensure that this valuable knowledge is accessible to all.

This book serves as a practical guide to using options for generating income, specifically focusing on strategies that can provide consistent returns in multiple trends. Whether you are new to options trading or an experienced trader seeking to improve your skills, this book will guide you through the process one step at a time.

First, we will analyze stocks from different perspectives. Understanding which stocks are worth trading and how the market moves is essential for developing a successful trading strategy. Next, we explore options: how they function, what influences their prices, and how to utilize them effectively. Finally, we will start combining options contracts to create credit spreads, positions where you are paid to enter the trade and are designed to profit from multiple market movements simultaneously. Yes, that's correct; you get paid to enter these trades.

We will discuss how to make money when the trades work and how to manage your trades when the market doesn't behave as expected. Finally, we will discuss how to transition to becoming a full-time options trader. Understanding why these strategies are effective and knowing when to use them is crucial for trading successfully. This book will guide you through each step, helping you avoid costly mistakes.

What sets this book apart is its foundation in real-world trading and practical application. By the time you finish, you won't just understand the terminology of options trading; you will also know how to use credit spreads to achieve your financial goals. Whether you aim to start a side hustle in your spare time or replace your current income, this book is written for you. You will learn how to reduce risk, maximize profit, and create the life you desire.

Here's how to get the most out of this book:

- **Go Step by Step:** Read the chapters in order, and don't skip the exercises at the end of each chapter. Even if you have experience trading options, I encourage you to start at the beginning; you might be surprised by what you learn. At the very least, you'll confirm what you already know and gain more confidence moving forward. However, you will likely discover that some of your long-held beliefs are incorrect and cause you to struggle unnecessarily.

- **Take Notes:** Write down what stands out to you, highlight key points, and practice the strategies with simulated trades before investing real money.
- **Stay Consistent:** Whether you dedicate a few minutes each day or set aside a specific time each week to read and practice, stick with it. Consistency is crucial to your success.

Are you ready to get started? Let's dive in!

CHAPTER 1

WHY SHOULD I TRADE OPTIONS?

EVERY DAY, PEOPLE WAKE up to noisy alarms, rush through their morning routines, and navigate through traffic, only to spend hours at jobs that leave them exhausted when they get home.

But imagine if your day looked like this:

You wake up whenever you're ready. You grab a coffee from your favorite spot and spend a few hours trading options on your laptop. The rest of the day is completely yours. And the best part is you're making more money doing this part-time than most people earn in their full-time jobs.

You are closer to making this a reality than you think.

Instead of being tied to a 9-to-5 job, options traders can trade whenever it suits them, from anywhere in the world. All you need is an internet connection, a computer, and knowledge. With options trading, your money works for you instead of the other way around.

Options provide a level of flexibility unmatched by other investments. With stocks, you only profit when the market rises. However, with options, you can earn returns whether the market is going up, down, or remaining flat. This versatility is what makes options so powerful.

While stocks and bonds typically grow slowly, options can yield larger returns in a shorter time frame and often with less risk. It's like driving your own car rather than waiting for a bus; you choose your destination and the speed at which you get there.

Options can help you manage risk effectively. They allow you to protect your stock investments and adjust your strategies based on market movements and your personal comfort with risk.

Why is this important? It's not just about making money; it's about gaining more control over your time and your future.

Imagine yourself at a coffee shop, enjoying your drink, when your phone buzzes with a notification that your trade has closed—and it turned a profit! It's not just the extra cash that brings a smile to your face; it's the freedom that comes with it.

Perhaps that money will cover your bills for the month, or maybe you're saving it for something bigger, like a down payment on a car, home repairs, or that long-awaited vacation. With every successful trade, you're gradually easing the financial stress that affects so many people.

And it's not just about your own financial health. It's also about creating a solid foundation for your family. Whether you're saving for your children's college education or simply preparing for unexpected expenses, you're building a sense of security that isn't reliant on your job.

Every trade brings you closer to your goals. It might feel far off, but you may be closer than you think.

Before you start trading, it's important to cover the basics. You need to learn how to select the right stocks and anticipate their price movements. While you don't have to predict the future with certainty, it's essential to understand how to identify trends. This book will teach you how to make money regardless of which direction the market moves, but you'll need some understanding of what to expect.

Let's begin by breaking down how the market operates. In the next chapter, I'll guide you through the factors that make a stock worth following and how to recognize when prices are about to change. By the time we finish, you'll be equipped to identify opportunities like a professional.

CHAPTER 2

MASTERING MARKET ANALYSIS

MARKET ANALYSIS IS THE foundation of any successful trading strategy, like a detailed roadmap guiding you through uncharted territory. You can uncover valuable clues about where the market might be headed by carefully examining the factors that impact asset prices, such as economic conditions, company performance, and broader market sentiment. This process goes beyond just following headlines or relying on intuition; it's about diving into the data to identify opportunities and avoid potential pitfalls.

Understanding trends, patterns, and key indicators allows you to anticipate market movements more precisely. Whether you're analyzing price charts, reviewing economic reports, or assessing trading volumes, each piece of information adds another layer to your decision-making process. When you consistently incorporate this analysis into your trading routine, you sharpen your ability to recognize profitable setups and avoid hasty moves that could lead to losses.

Ultimately, market analysis empowers you to trade with confidence rather than speculation. It shifts your approach from reactive to proactive, enabling you to act decisively when opportunities arise. With a strong grasp of market dynamics, you're better equipped to navigate the complexities of trading, increase your odds of success, and achieve your financial goals over time.

2.1 Fundamental Analysis: Finding Good Stocks

Navigating the world of stocks can be overwhelming, especially with so many companies and millions of shares traded daily. But don't worry; I'm here to simplify the process for you!

We'll focus on U.S. equities, which are governed by clear regulations and enjoy a high trading volume, creating ample opportunities. When I mention "equities," I'm referring to stocks, Exchange-Traded Funds (ETFs), indexes, and Real Estate Investment Trusts (REITs). While options can also be traded on commodities and futures, our main focus will be on the equity market. So, for now, let's concentrate on that area.

Building a Watchlist

Instead of constantly chasing the market and seeking new stocks to trade each day, a more effective approach is to create a watchlist of equities you are familiar with and focus on trading strategies that align with those stocks in the current market conditions. Sticking to a smaller group of stocks allows you to understand them better. Over time, you'll start to notice patterns and discern how they behave at specific times, such as around earnings announcements or during different seasons. It's similar to knowing a person well; it becomes easier to anticipate their actions.

Begin by analyzing 10 to 15 stocks and choose a few for active trading. Start small and gradually expand the number of stocks you follow as your comfort and skill level increase.

Don't worry about making your watchlist permanent; you can adjust it whenever necessary. Feel free to add new stocks, remove those that aren't performing well, and keep it flexible.

So, how do you decide which stocks to keep on your watchlist? Let's explore that.

Digging Into Financial Health

Researching stocks involves more than just looking at their price. It's important to dig deeper to understand how the company is actually performing. This means examining factors such as the level of trading activity for the stock, the concentration of ownership among major investors, the timing of earnings reports, and the company's debt levels. All of this information helps you assess whether the company is financially healthy and if it's a worthy investment opportunity.

Trading Volume

When trading activity is high, it becomes easier to enter and exit trades. However, if trading volume is low, you may encounter challenges when attempting to buy or sell your positions. It is advisable to focus on stocks that have at least one million shares traded each day.

Additionally, it's important to assess the options volume for those stocks. Look for indications of high trading activity and open interest, which refers to the number of outstanding contracts that have not yet been settled. Both of these factors reflect the level of activity in the options market for a given stock.

You can find this information on websites like Yahoo Finance, Bloomberg, and MarketWatch.

Institutional Ownership

Large investors, such as mutual funds, hedge funds, and pension funds, invest significant amounts of money in the stock market. But why should this concern you?

When many institutional investors hold shares in a particular company, it generally indicates that they have thoroughly researched and identified value in that company. These organizations often have dedicated teams responsible for conducting due diligence to evaluate potential investments.

If over 50% of a company's stock is owned by institutional investors, it serves as a strong vote of confidence, suggesting that the stock is likely to perform well.

However, when these institutions buy shares of a company's stock, it can significantly drive up the price. Conversely, if these large investors begin selling their shares, it may signal potential issues with the company, leading to a rapid decline in the stock price.

Earnings Dates

Public companies release their earnings reports every quarter, providing valuable information about their financial performance. These reports include details on the company's revenue, profits, and future expectations. Earnings reports can significantly influence a stock's price, so it's important to stay informed about when they are scheduled.

Earnings dates are announced in advance, so they should never take you by surprise. You can easily track earnings dates on websites like Yahoo Finance or Bloomberg, and you can also set up alerts through your brokerage.

Some trades are suitable to hold over earnings reports, while others are not. Make sure you know the next earnings report date before entering any trade.

Valuation Techniques

There are several tools you can use to figure out if a stock is worth its price. The Price-to-Earnings (P/E) ratio and the Price-to-Book (P/B) ratio are two big ones. They help you see if a stock might be undervalued (potentially a good deal) or overpriced (something to be cautious of).

But don't just look at the number; dig deeper to understand the data's story. The same information could be a result of different causes. For example, a low P/E ratio might mean the stock is a bargain, or it could signal that the company has some issues.

A company with a high price-to-earnings (P/E) ratio needs to demonstrate significantly large growth rates to justify its elevated stock price. During bearish market periods, stocks characterized as "speculative" due to their high P/E ratios often experience greater price declines compared to equities with more reasonable P/E ratios.

Sector and Industry Analysis

Understanding the sectors and industries that your stocks belong to is crucial, as it can significantly impact their performance. Economic factors, technological advancements, regulations, and competition all influence how stocks behave.

For example, when the Federal Reserve raises interest rates, it may benefit banks but negatively affect the housing market. Similarly, a new technological breakthrough can positively impact companies in that sector, such as the rise of electric vehicles, which has influenced automotive manufacturers and battery suppliers.

Staying Informed

To stay competitive, it's essential to keep updated with the latest news and trends in your sectors. The more informed you are, the better you'll predict market movements and adjust your portfolio.

Short-Term vs. Long-Term Impact

Understanding the difference between short-term and long-term impacts can help you remain calm when stock prices fluctuate quickly, as these movements may not significantly affect the overall picture. By mastering these fundamentals, you set yourself up to make smarter trades and avoid unpleasant surprises. The more proficient you become at stock analysis, the more confident you will feel in your decisions, aligning them more closely with your financial goals. For example, a low P/E ratio could indicate that a stock is a good deal; however, it might also serve as a warning sign that the company has some underlying issues.

A valuable resource for conducting thorough due diligence is the Securities and Exchange Commission website: www.sec.gov.

2.2 Technical Analysis 101: Reading Charts and Patterns

Consider the task of predicting the weather for a trip you're planning. Fundamental analysis is akin to studying long-term weather patterns, understanding the landscape, and examining how the seasons affect the area. You gather all the big-picture factors that influence the weather to ensure you don't end up in your tropical paradise during hurricane season.

In contrast, if you were trying to predict tomorrow's weather, you might glance at the sky, feel the wind, and check a barometer. Your guess would rely on experience and your knowledge of the seasons. You could make some general assumptions, and sometimes you'd be right, but the accuracy would be limited. Now, imagine you had a weather app that utilizes historical data, recognizes patterns, and employs smart algorithms to provide a forecast. This is similar to how technical analysis operates in trading.

With fundamental analysis, you examine a company's overall financial health, management, and market position. You focus on the factors that affect the long-term viability of the equity. On the other hand, technical analysis helps you identify short-term trends and spot opportunities in the market by analyzing price charts and trading volumes.

Before we dive into technical analysis, it's important to remember the foundation you've already built. Having a solid understanding of fundamental analysis is crucial. It helps you grasp a company's true value, its financial health, and the overall market conditions. Think of it like knowing whether it's usually rainy, dry, hot, or cold in a certain area. Once you have that understanding, technical analysis allows you to zoom in and make more specific predictions—adding short-term forecasts to your general weather knowledge.

Technical analysis removes much of the guesswork from trading and helps you develop a more strategic approach. It enables you to spot trends and patterns that might not be immediately obvious. It's like moving from simply checking the wind with your finger to having a fully equipped weather station. You're no longer just guessing; you have data backing you up to help you make smarter decisions.

However, no method is foolproof. Just as weather forecasts can sometimes be inaccurate, even the best technical analysis can occasionally lead you astray. Markets can change rapidly due to news, events, or unpredictable human behavior—factors that charts can't always capture. That's why it's essential to use technical analysis alongside other tools in your trading strategy and to always be prepared for surprises.

In this chapter, we will break down the core tools and techniques of technical analysis. By the end, you'll be equipped to trade more confidently, using these insights to sharpen your strategy and work toward your financial goals.

Chart Types and Setups

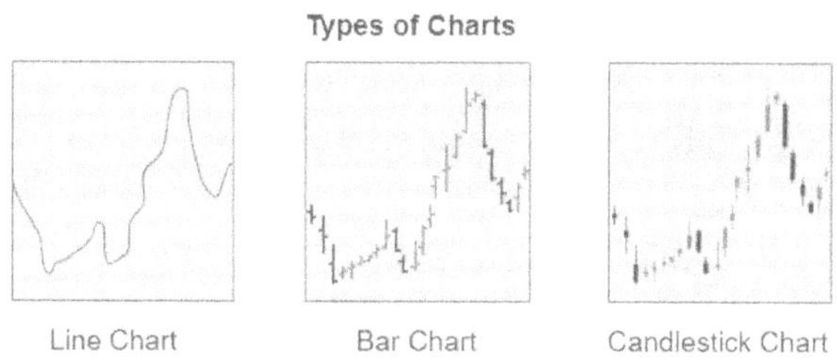

When looking at historical stock data, there are three main types of charts to consider: line charts, bar charts, and candlestick charts.

Line charts are the simplest of the three. They plot the closing prices over time, allowing you to observe the general movement of a stock's price. These charts are great for getting a quick overview of the price trend.

Bar charts provide more information. In addition to showing the closing price, they also display the opening price, the highest and lowest points, and the closing price for each period. This additional information helps you gain a clearer understanding of how the price fluctuates throughout the day.

Candlestick charts offer even more detail, presented in a visually intuitive format. The body of the candlestick represents the opening and closing prices, while the wicks indicate the highest and lowest points for that period. The colors—typically red and green—make it easy to see whether the price closed higher or lower than it opened, simplifying the task of spotting patterns and trends.

Understanding and Identifying Trends

Recognizing trends is one of the most important aspects of trading. A trend is simply the general direction in which the market or a stock is moving. There are three main trends to watch for uptrends, downtrends, and sideways (or range-bound) trends.

An **uptrend** indicates that prices are generally increasing over time, characterized by higher highs and higher lows. Think of it as climbing a hill, with some dips along the way. On the other hand, a **downtrend** is the opposite, with lower highs and lower lows resembling a slow downhill slope. **Sideways trends** occur when prices remain relatively stable, bouncing up and down within a specific range.

Identifying these trends early is crucial, as it provides insight into where prices may be headed next. It also helps in selecting strategies that align with the prevailing trend.

Stock prices can experience significant changes between trading sessions, which is referred to as a gap. Stocks can gap up, rising to a higher value, or gap down, falling to a lower level. These substantial movements often occur due to news or earnings reports and may indicate the start of a new trend.

Support and Resistance

Support and resistance levels serve as invisible barriers in the market. Support is the price level at which a stock typically stops declining because buyers enter the market. On the other hand, resistance is where a stock usually stops rising as investors begin to sell off.

Identifying these levels can help you predict when the price might reverse. Understanding these key points makes it easier to secure profits and can be particularly beneficial when using trading strategies like credit spreads.

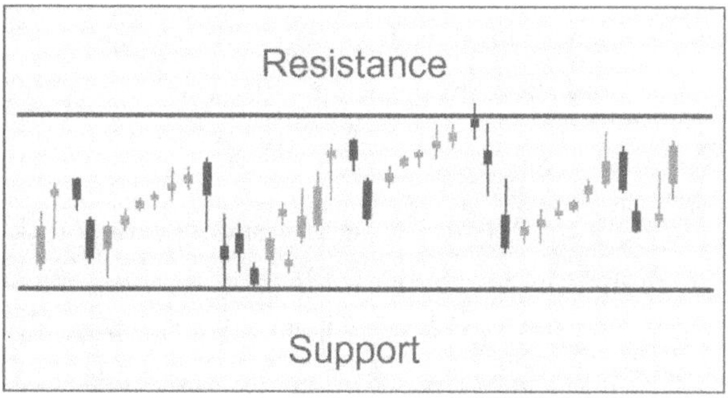

To identify these levels, examine a stock's recent chart. **Support** occurs where the price rebounds after reaching a low, while **resistance** is found at the peak, where the price recedes.

Key Technical Indicators

If you're looking to enhance your trading strategies, technical indicators can be incredibly helpful. They provide insights into potential market movements. However, with the multitude of indicators available, it's easy to feel overwhelmed. Many new traders attempt to analyze everything simultaneously and can become confused about where to concentrate their efforts. It's crucial to remember that all indicators are merely tools; there isn't a guaranteed combination that can predict the future with 100% accuracy. That's why I focus on three key indicators that I find most beneficial.

The RSI (Relative Strength Index) is useful for identifying overbought or oversold conditions. If the RSI exceeds 70, the stock may be considered overbought and likely to pull back. Conversely, if it's below 30, the stock may be oversold and poised for a bounce.

The MACD (Moving Average Convergence Divergence) is effective for detecting changes in the strength and direction of a trend. A bullish signal occurs when the MACD line crosses above the signal line, while a bearish signal occurs when it crosses below.

The EMA (Exponential Moving Average) responds more quickly to price changes than a simple moving average. For instance, when the 5-day EMA crosses above the 20-day EMA, it typically indicates an upward trend. Conversely, if the 5-day EMA crosses below the 20-day EMA, it signals a downward trend.

It's important not to rely on just one indicator. The best outcomes are achieved when all three indicators—RSI, MACD, and EMA—converge. When this alignment occurs, they reinforce each other and enhance your confidence in your predictions.

As you become more familiar with charts, you'll begin to recognize patterns that provide insights into potential price movements. Identifying these patterns early can offer a significant advantage, allowing you to act before the market changes.

Not a Crystal Ball

Just because something worked in the past doesn't mean it will always work the same way in the future. That's why it's important to combine technical analysis with fundamental analysis, smart risk management, and a commitment to continuous learning. While technical analysis can be a great tool, you need to use it in context and apply some common sense to truly maximize its potential.

2.3 Sentimental Analysis: Gauging Market Emotions

News can change the market in an instant. **Market sentiment** reflects how investors feel—whether they have a positive or negative outlook on a stock or the market as a whole. While it's hard to measure sentiment precisely, it significantly influences prices. Generally, when people are confident, prices tend to rise; when they are worried, prices usually fall. For instance, if investors believe a company has a promising future, they will start buying shares, driving the price higher.

Major news events can quickly alter public sentiment about the market. Scandals, for example, can lead to a sharp decline in a stock's price. Elections often introduce uncertainty, prompting market fluctuations as traders speculate on potential outcomes. Additionally, events such as wars or political tensions can cause investors to withdraw their money from stocks and shift it into safer assets like bonds, typically resulting in lower stock prices.

Tools for Measuring Sentiment

Although sentiment cannot be measured directly, several tools can help gauge it. One popular tool is the **Volatility Index (VIX)**, which tracks the expected volatility of the market based on options for the S&P 500. Often referred to as the "fear gauge," a rising VIX indicates that investors are feeling nervous, while a declining VIX suggests increased confidence.

Another useful tool is the **put/call ratio**, which compares the number of bearish put options being traded to bullish call options. A high put ratio indicates that more investors are betting against the market, signaling bearish sentiment. Conversely, a low ratio suggests that investors are feeling positive and anticipate a market rise.

Additionally, **sentiment surveys** can provide insights into how investors feel about the market, both in the short and long term. These surveys offer a quick overview of whether sentiment is optimistic or fearful.

Interpreting Sentiment Data

Instead of focusing on just one piece of sentiment data, it's helpful to step back and see how everything fits together. For instance, a spike in the VIX (Volatility Index) typically indicates that investors are becoming worried, possibly due to bad news or a weak economic report. Conversely, a low VIX may suggest that investors are feeling overly relaxed, which can sometimes precede a market correction.

The put/call ratio provides similar insights. If the ratio is increasing, it signals that more investors are becoming bearish. On the other hand, if the ratio is decreasing, it may indicate that investors are starting to feel more optimistic, suggesting that the market could be poised for a rebound.

Sentiment analysis is most effective when combined with other tools, such as technical and fundamental analysis. For example, if your fundamental analysis shows that a stock is undervalued and sentiment is positive, it could be an ideal time to adopt a bullish strategy, such as bull put spreads. Conversely, if sentiment is more negative, bearish strategies like bear call spreads might be more appropriate.

Monitoring the news, observing public reactions, and tracking market trends can provide insight into future developments. It's important to balance market emotions with data to make more informed trading decisions. By integrating sentiment analysis with technical and fundamental analysis, you can improve your chances of staying ahead in the market.

2.4 Incorporating Economic Events into Market Analysis

When you're trading, it's important to recognize that there's more to it than simply tracking the stock market. Factors such as the economy, business developments, and political events can all influence market behavior and the performance of your trades.

Economic indicators like GDP growth, unemployment rates, and inflation provide a general overview of the economy's health. A rising GDP typically signals a strong economy, which often leads to higher stock prices. Conversely, high unemployment can result in decreased consumer spending, causing the market to decline. Inflation is also a significant factor, as it affects interest rates, which have a direct impact on stock prices.

Major global events and political changes can create volatility in the market. For example, new trade agreements or government policies might benefit some industries while posing challenges for others. Events such as wars, international agreements, or shifts in currency exchange rates can affect the prices of essential goods like oil and food, potentially disrupting your trading strategy.

You don't need to stay glued to the news all day to stay informed. Platforms like Bloomberg and Reuters provide real-time updates, while apps like X (formerly Twitter) allow you to quickly access breaking news. You can also set up Google

Alerts for specific stocks or industries to ensure you don't miss any critical updates.

By monitoring the environment around you, you can anticipate changes and adjust your trading strategy accordingly.

2.5 Tools and Resources for Effective Market Analysis

With today's technology, you have instant access to a wealth of information. Whether you're on your computer or using your phone, there are numerous platforms and apps available that can help you track the market, identify trends, and make informed decisions.

It's easier than ever to view real-time data, analyze charts, and learn as you go. These tools enable you to stay updated on the market and make smarter trades. Utilizing the right resources can help you make quicker decisions and stay ahead in this fast-paced environment.

Software and Platforms

There are many options available to help you analyze the market. **TradingView** is a popular platform known for its charts and features that allow traders to share their ideas. You can start with the free version or opt for a paid subscription to access additional features, such as more comprehensive data.

MetaTrader is another reliable choice, commonly used by forex and futures traders, but it is also effective for stock trading.

Thinkorswim by Schwab offers detailed tools along with a wealth of educational content to help you enhance your skills.

Mobile Apps

If you enjoy trading on the go, mobile apps can be very beneficial. **E*TRADE Mobile** offers real-time quotes and user-friendly charts, allowing you to make trades directly from your phone. **Robinhood** is particularly popular among beginners due to its simplicity and the absence of commission fees. For more experienced traders, **Interactive Brokers** provides an app packed with advanced tools, including risk management features and research data.

These tools are designed to assist you, not to make decisions on your behalf. As you become more comfortable using them, you'll gain a better understanding of the market, allowing you to make more confident trades.

2.6 Developing a Routine for Market Analysis

Establishing a regular routine for market analysis is essential for staying informed and making smarter trading decisions. Like any other habit, consistency leads to better results. Whether you are focused on day trading or long-term investments, having a routine helps you stay organized and on track.

Setting Goals

Begin by determining what you want from your daily routine. Are you concentrating on quick trades, or are you more interested in observing longer-term trends? Perhaps you simply want to monitor certain stocks or ensure that your portfolio remains within your risk tolerance. When you have clear goals, it becomes easier to focus on what truly matters.

Gathering the Right Information

Next, collect only the information that is relevant to your trades. With an abundance of data available, it's easy to feel overwhelmed. Focus on tools that provide updates specifically for the stocks you care about. Utilize financial news alerts or set up notifications for significant price changes. Apps can assist you in filtering out unnecessary information and delivering the insights that matter most.

Breaking Down the Data

Once you've gathered your data, simplify the analysis. Start by checking the fundamentals: How is the company performing? Is the industry moving in a positive direction? Next, examine the charts. Utilize tools such as moving averages or indicators like the Relative Strength Index (RSI) to determine if a stock may be overbought or oversold. By piecing all of this information together, you'll gain a clearer understanding of the situation.

Adapting to Changes

Markets can be unpredictable, so it's important to stay alert. Monitor your stocks closely, and if you notice any shifts, don't hesitate to adjust your risk.

During chaotic market conditions, it may be wise to take a step back and wait for things to stabilize. Being flexible allows you to identify good opportunities without feeling rushed.

Your routine should align with your investment style and help you stay on track. Remain consistent, but be prepared to make adjustments when circumstances change.

2.7 Test Your Knowledge

You've conducted extensive market analysis, so take a moment to identify what really stands out. It's not enough to simply know the facts; you need to apply them in your trades. I have some questions to help you reflect on how this knowledge translates into real-world situations. These questions are designed to assist you in applying what you've learned to actual trading scenarios.

Chapter Quiz

- Why should you consider a company's debt-to-equity ratio when assessing its financial health?
- How does the put/call ratio provide insight into market sentiment, and what might a high ratio indicate about investors' feelings?
- If a company exceeds expectations in its earnings report, how could this impact its stock price and options premiums?

- How can moving averages assist you in determining the optimal time to enter a bullish options trade?
- Why is it important to understand both technical and fundamental analysis?
- How can sentiment analysis guide your decision-making between bullish and bearish strategies?

These questions are designed to help you apply your knowledge to make better trading decisions. Reflecting on them will enhance your skills and provide you with a more experienced perspective on the market.

Practical Application

Let's put this knowledge to work! Try these three exercises to start turning theory into practical skills for your trading:

1. **Build a Watchlist:** Choose five companies from different industries and track their performance for a month. Monitor their stock prices daily, note any significant news, and observe how their prices react. This will help you understand how various sectors move and how external events influence stock prices.
2. **Do a Deep Dive:** Select one of the companies from your watchlist and conduct a comprehensive fundamental analysis. Examine the financial statements, look into key ratios such as price-to-earnings (P/E), price-to-book (P/B), and debt-to-equity, and assess the company's position in the market. Ultimately, determine whether you believe the

stock is overpriced, underpriced, or fairly valued.

3. **Test Your Technical Analysis:** Use the historical data of one stock from your watchlist to identify trends, patterns, and support and resistance levels. Apply a few technical indicators to speculate whether the stock's trend will continue or reverse, then track it to evaluate the accuracy of your predictions. This exercise will enhance your technical analysis skills and boost your confidence in applying them.

By completing these exercises, you'll transform the theory you've learned into practical skills. The more you practice, the more everything will start to click!

CHAPTER 3

FOUNDATIONS FOR SMART OPTIONS TRADING

MANY PEOPLE MISTAKENLY BELIEVE that options trading is akin to gambling, but this view is far from accurate. Options were designed as tools to manage risk in financial markets, not as a form of casino entertainment. While there are certainly risky ways to utilize options, when used properly, they are primarily about managing risk rather than taking chances. For instance, an airline might use options to hedge against the risk of skyrocketing fuel prices.

The first step you should take is to learn the terminology associated with options trading. For those new to the field, it can feel like entering a crowded room where everyone is speaking a language you don't understand, and everything seems to be happening at once.

However, just as you would learn some essential phrases before visiting a new country, understanding the language of options trading is the critical first step to feeling at ease. You wouldn't embark on a trip to Paris without knowing how to order coffee or ask for directions, right? The same principle applies here.

This chapter will serve as your guide to unraveling the language of options trading. By the end, you will feel much more confident and prepared to enter the options market with solid knowledge.

3.1 Terminology: Understanding the Language of Options

Let's go over some common terms you'll run into when trading options.

Every options contract has a buyer and a seller. Pretty straightforward, right? If you buy something, someone's selling it. And if you're selling, someone's got to buy it from you.

Long Options: If you're "long" on an option, it means you bought the option contract. You have the right to exercise it anytime before it expires.

Short Options: Being "short" on an option means you sold the option contract. If the buyer decides to use it, you're responsible for honoring the deal.

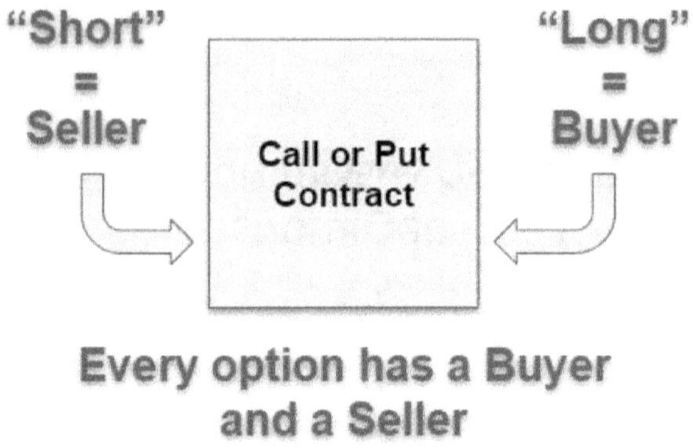

Strike Price: This is the agreed price for buying or selling the asset if the option is exercised.

Expiration Date: Every option has an end date. If you don't use the option by this date, it's useless, like an expired coupon.

Option Premium: This is the price you pay to buy an option or the amount you get if you sell one.

Exercise: When the buyer uses their option rights.

Assignment: This is when the option buyer exercises and the seller has to complete the deal.

In-the-money (ITM): If exercising the option would give you a profit, it's "in-the-money." For calls, this means the asset price is above the strike price. For puts, the asset price is lower.

At-the-money (ATM): The asset price matches the strike price right in the middle. A small move could put it in-the-money or out-of-the-money.

Out-of-the-money (OTM): If exercising the option wouldn't result in a profit, it's out-of-the-money. For calls, the asset's price is below the strike price. For puts, the price is higher.

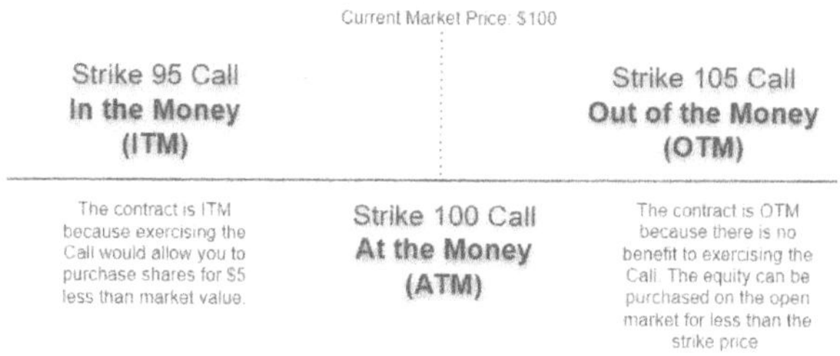

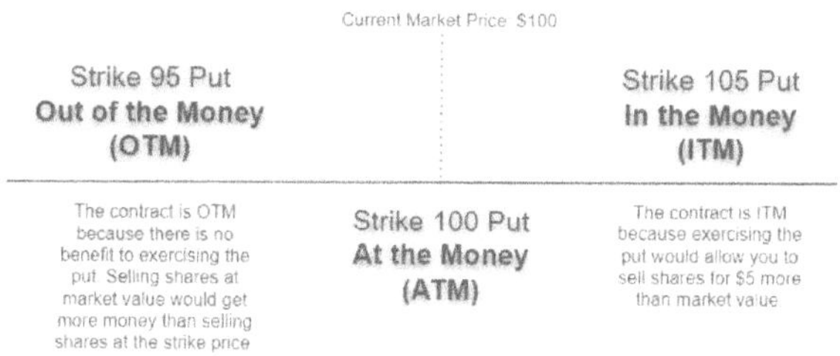

These terms might seem like a lot at first, but once you get them down, it's like having a map to make sense of it all. They'll definitely come in handy when you're talking with other traders or planning your next moves.

Try It Out

Here's a quick way to practice:

1. Find a financial news article or check out the stock market section.
2. Look for mentions of options and see if you can spot these terms.
3. Figure out how they're being used and how they connect to what's happening in the market.

The more you use these terms, the easier they'll get. Work them into your analysis and conversations, and before long, they'll feel natural.

3.2 Calls and Puts: The Building Blocks of Options Trading

Alright, now we're getting to the really exciting part. With the basic vocabulary under your belt, we can dive into options trading. At its core, an option is a contract that gives you the right, but not the obligation, to buy or sell 100 shares of an underlying asset at a set price before a certain date. Options let you control more shares with less money upfront, which limits your risk but can boost your potential return. This flexibility and potential for big gains is what makes options trading appealing to many traders.

There are two types of options: calls and puts. Let's start by looking at calls.

Long Calls

Let's say you've been eyeing tickets for a concert by your favorite band. You think ticket prices are going to soar as the concert date gets closer. Instead of paying full price now, you pay a small fee to reserve the right to buy the tickets later at today's price, no matter how high they get next month. If the prices go down, you've only lost a small fee. But if they jump, you can either buy the tickets at a lower price or sell your spot to someone else. Either way, you're happy you locked in that low price.

A call option works the same way. You pay a premium to lock in the price of a stock you think will go up. If the price rises, you can either exercise your option to buy the stock at the agreed price or sell the call to someone else who wants those shares.

Here's an example of a long call: You're interested in a tech stock trading at $100, and you expect the price to go up. Buying 100 shares outright would cost you $10,000. But instead, you could buy a call option. Let's say you spend $2 per share ($200 per contract) to buy a slightly out-of-the-money long call at a $105 strike price. This option gives you control over 100 shares, even though you haven't bought them, and your risk is capped at the $200 you paid.

The company has released a game-changing new product, and the stock has shot up to $120. Now you've got choices.

1. **Exercise the Call Option:** You could exercise your option and buy the 100 shares at $105 each. Including the $2 per share premium, your total cost per share is $107. You could sell the shares at $120 or hold onto them for the long term.

2. **Sell the Call Option:** As the stock price rises, so does the value of your call option. Instead of exercising, you could sell the call for a profit. At this point, your call has an intrinsic value of $15 per share or $1,500 per contract. Selling the call would give you a $1,300 profit from your $200 investment, an impressive 650% return!

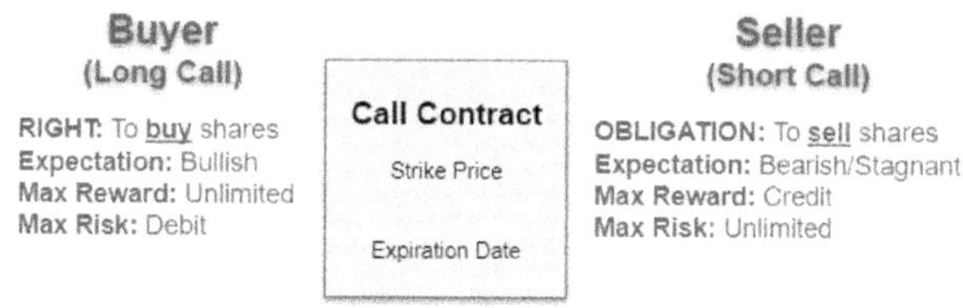

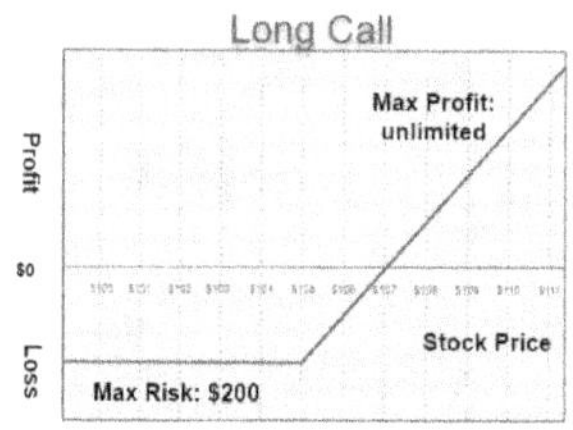

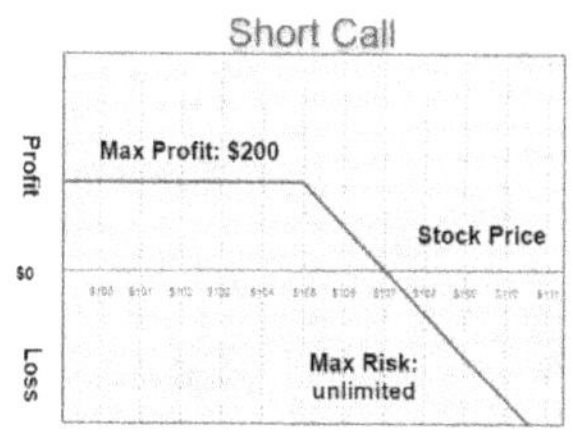

In this example, the stock went up by 20%. If you had bought the stock outright, you would have made a 20% profit. But by purchasing the call option for $200 and selling it for $1,500, you made $1,300, a 650% return on your investment. This leverage is one of the reasons options are so popular.

Short Calls

Now, let's look at the same call from the seller's perspective. The seller collected a $200 premium upfront. If they already own the shares (a covered call strategy), they keep any stock gains up to the $105 strike price. If the stock stays below $105, they get to keep the shares and the premium. However, if the stock goes above $105, they must sell the shares at the strike price, limiting their potential profits.

If the stock price jumps to $120, the seller is forced to sell 100 shares at $105. They still keep the $200 premium and any gains up to $105, but they miss out on the additional $15 of appreciation.

Covered calls are a strategy often used by investors who think the stock will stay flat or rise slightly. It's a way to generate income while holding onto the stock or to exit a long position.

Pro Tip:

Selling naked calls (short calls without owning the underlying shares or using a spread to limit risk) is a high-risk strategy. The higher the stock price, the more the seller loses, and there's no limit to how high a stock can climb, so the risk is potentially unlimited.
This is why selling naked calls is considered one of the riskiest strategies. Without owning the shares or having a spread in place, you're exposed to unlimited losses.

Long Puts

Let's dive into puts. Think of a long put like insurance for your investments. Just like you wouldn't drive without car insurance, you shouldn't hold a stock without a way to protect it from losing value.

Take car insurance: you pay a little upfront to protect yourself from a big financial hit if something goes wrong. A put option works the same way for stocks. You pay a premium for the right to sell shares at a set price. If the stock price drops, you can sell your shares at a higher price and avoid taking a loss.

Here's an example: Let's say a company's stock is trading at $80, but you're worried the price might drop. Normally, you'd avoid buying the stock until the price falls. But with a put option, you can actually make money if the price goes down.

You buy a put with an $80 strike price, paying $1.50 per share ($150 total). The company announces bad news, and the stock drops to $60. Now, you've got options:

1. **Exercise the Put:** You can buy 100 shares at $60 and then use your put to sell them at $80, making $20 per share ($2,000 total).

2. **Sell the Put:** As the stock price drops, your put increases in value. Instead of using the option, you could sell it for $20 per share, making a $2,000 profit without having to buy or sell the stock.

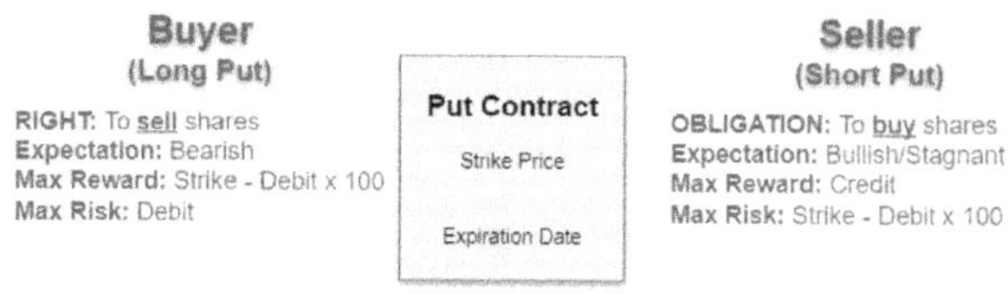

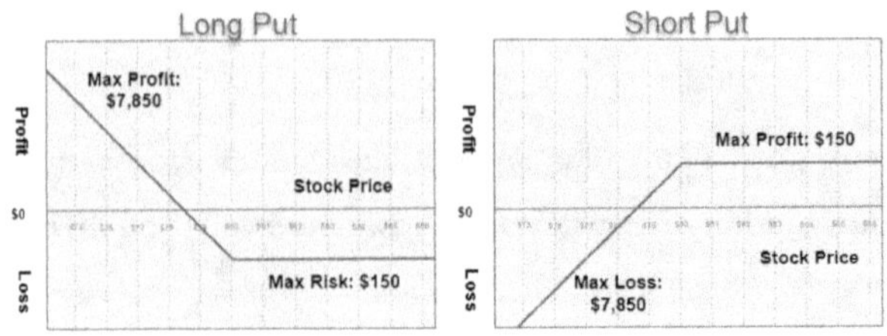

That's what makes put options so handy. They give you a way to shield your portfolio, or even profit, when prices fall, kind of like having insurance.

Short Puts

Now, let's flip things around and talk about selling puts. The seller collects $150 upfront for selling a put. They've basically sold an insurance policy, agreeing to take the stock if it drops below $80.

If the stock falls to $60, the seller has to buy 100 shares at $80. After factoring in the $1.50 premium they got, their cost is $78.50 per share, meaning they're down $18.50 per share.

But this isn't always a bad thing for the seller. If they're confident in the stock's long-term potential, they might be okay holding on and waiting for the price to rebound. In some cases, they might've sold the put because they actually wanted to own the stock anyway. Plus, selling covered calls on those shares could bring in extra income.

	Bullish	Bearish
Puts	**Short Put** Sell to Open *Obligation* to **Buy** Shares	**Long Put** Buy to Open *Right* to **Sell** Shares

Strategic Implications

Trading options is all about juggling immediate cash with possible future gains or losses. It's like deciding between a paycheck today or the possibility of a bigger payday later.

When you buy a call option, you're making a small bet with the hope of a big return. When you sell a call, you're taking guaranteed income now but giving up some future upside.

Put options are a bit different. When you buy a put, you're buying protection, just like insurance. You hope you won't need it, but it's there if things go south. When you sell a put, you're collecting income now, but you're taking the risk of having to buy the stock if the price drops.

Covered calls and selling puts are great ways to bring in income when the market is neutral or slightly bullish, but they do require capital. You need the stock for covered calls, and you need cash on hand to buy the stock if you sell puts. Both strategies can leave you exposed to big losses if the market tanks.

You can trade these strategies on their own, or you can combine them to create more complex positions. In fact, all of the "advanced" options strategies you hear about are just combinations of these basic moves.

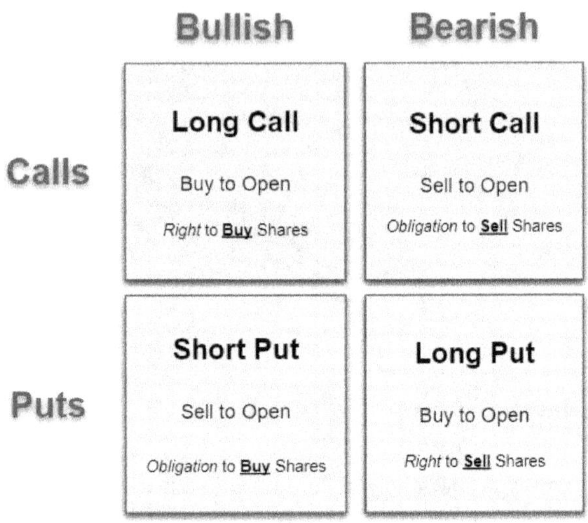

Later on, I'll show you how to use options in ways that let you achieve the same goals as covered calls and short puts but with less money tied up and lower risk. Stick around. The best is yet to come!

Understanding Strike Price and Expiration Dates

Two key things that can make or break your trades are the strike price and expiration date of your options. The strike price is simply the price at which the option holder can buy or sell the asset. Picking the right strike price is crucial because it directly affects how profitable your trade could be.

Choosing the right strike price depends on your strategy and involves looking at current market conditions and your goals. For example, if you think a stock is going to shoot up, you might pick a strike price just above the current market price (this is called "out of the money") when buying a call. You're betting the stock will go higher than that price before the option expires. On the other hand, if you want to play it safe, you might go for an "at the money" strike price (where the strike price matches the current price) for a better balance between cost and potential return. If you're more aggressive, you might pick an "in the money" strike price (below the current price) to maximize potential gains if the stock rises, but remember; this also increases your risk if the stock drops. The main thing is to make sure your choice fits your risk tolerance and market view instead of just going with what some online guru says.

The expiration date is the day your option contract expires, it's the deadline for deciding what to do with your option. If you hold a long option, this is your last chance to exercise it, sell it, or let it expire. If you're holding a short option, it's your final opportunity to buy it back, let it get assigned, or let it expire. The expiration date matters because it sets the window for your trade to work out.

Short-term options are cheaper and can lead to quick wins if the market moves fast, but you've only got a small time frame for things to go your way. Long-term options cost more but give you more breathing room for the stock to make its move, and they can be less stressful to manage.

Smart traders use expiration dates to their advantage by picking options that expire further out in the future. This gives their trades more time to develop and gives them room to adjust if things don't go as planned. For instance, if you're banking on a company making a big announcement next week, a short-term option might seem like a good idea because you're expecting a quick spike. But if the news doesn't live up to the hype or gets delayed, that option could expire worthless.

On the flip side, choosing an option with a later expiration date gives you time to react if things don't go as expected, and you can still benefit if the price jumps later. This flexibility is especially helpful in volatile markets. If you're focused on long-term trends, like a tech boom or economic recovery, long-term options give your trade time to grow.

Keep in mind that you don't have to hold options until they expire. If the market moves in your favor earlier than expected, you can close your position and lock in profits. That flexibility is one of the biggest perks of trading options and can help you make smarter decisions.

3.3 Option Pricing

One of the most well-known models for figuring out option prices is the Black-Scholes model. Think of it like a chef's secret recipe for finding the fair price of an option. Developed in the early 1970s by Fischer Black, Myron Scholes, and Robert Merton, this model has become a go-to for options pricing in modern trading.

At its core, the Black-Scholes model gives a theoretical estimate of the price of European-style options, which can only be exercised at expiration. The model takes into account several key factors:

- **Current Stock Price:** The current price of the underlying asset is where it all starts.
- **Strike Price:** This is the price at which you can buy or sell the underlying asset when the option expires.
- **Time to Expiration:** How much time is left before the option runs out.
- **Volatility:** How much the price of the underlying asset is expected to fluctuate.
- **Risk-Free Interest Rate:** Usually based on government bonds, this

reflects the time value of money.

The Black-Scholes formula mixes these inputs to come up with a fair price for the option. While the actual math behind it is pretty complicated, involving things like differential equations and standard normal distribution functions, the big takeaway is that it helps traders figure out whether an option is priced too high or too low based on market conditions.

The beauty of the Black-Scholes model is that it gives traders a standardized way to price options. If the market price of an option is higher than the Black-Scholes estimate, it could be overvalued, which might present a selling opportunity. If it's lower, the option could be undervalued, making it a good time to buy.

In practice, traders use the Black-Scholes model as a starting point. They often tweak the inputs to better reflect real-time market conditions, like changes in volatility. Even though the model has some limitations, like assuming constant volatility and interest rates, it's still a key tool for options traders.

Now, do you need to fully understand the Black-Scholes model to be a successful options trader? Not really, and here's why.

While it's a great tool for pricing European options, which can only be exercised at expiration, most options traded in the U.S. are American-style, meaning they can be exercised at any time before expiration. The Black-Scholes model doesn't perfectly account for that flexibility, which is why traders often use other models, like the Binomial Options Pricing model, for American options. But here's the good news: you don't need to dive into complicated formulas to trade well.

What really matters is understanding the market, making smart decisions, and managing your risk. The Black-Scholes model gives you a framework for how options are priced, but you won't need to crunch the numbers yourself. Most trading platforms handle the heavy lifting, giving you real-time option prices based on various models.

Think of it like driving a car. You don't need to know exactly how the engine works to drive safely. You just need to know how to operate the car, follow the rules, and adapt to changing road conditions. It's the same with options trading, you need to know how to analyze market conditions, manage your trades, and adjust your strategies as needed.

So, while the Black-Scholes model is an important part of options theory, you don't need to be a math expert to trade successfully. Focus on what really counts:

- Learn how to read market data and trends.
- Use the tools and resources available to you.
- Stick to a solid trading strategy.
- Understand how to manage risk.

By sticking to the practical stuff, you'll be able to navigate options trading smoothly and still benefit from models like Black-Scholes without getting bogged down in the complicated math. Trading is a mix of both art and science and with the right approach, you can get really good at it.

For now, we'll focus on the factors that affect the price of call and put options so you can get a feel for how an option's value might change as the market moves without needing to solve complicated math equations.

What You Need to Know

There are several factors that affect the value of an options contract. Think of it like peeling an onion; each layer adds to the overall picture. The price of the underlying asset is the most obvious one. As the stock moves closer to the option's strike price, the option's value generally goes up. Volatility also plays a big part; the more volatile the stock, the higher the chance it'll hit the strike price, which increases the option's value. Time decay is another critical factor. As an option gets closer to its expiration date, its value tends to drop, all else being equal. Finally, interest rates can have an impact, though they usually play a more subtle role compared to other factors.

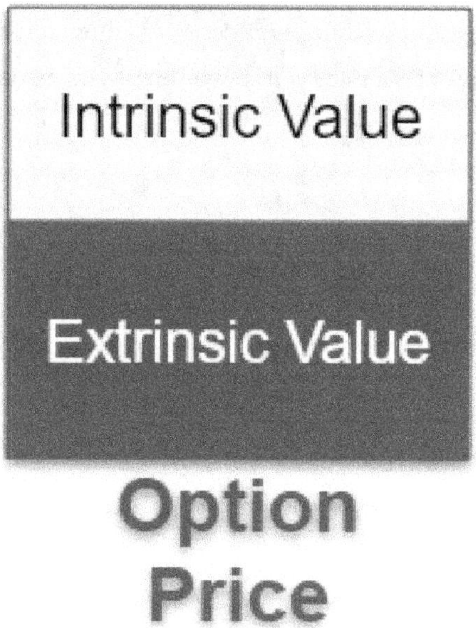

3.4 Intrinsic vs Extrinsic Value

When you look at an option's total value, the price you pay or receive when trading, it can be split into two parts: intrinsic and extrinsic value. Every option has extrinsic value until it expires, but only in-the-money options have intrinsic value. Intrinsic value is what the option is worth if you were to exercise it right now. If exercising wouldn't make sense, like buying above the market price or selling below it, the intrinsic value is zero.

Extrinsic value is the extra amount traders are willing to pay over the intrinsic value based on future expectations and the time left until expiration. It's essentially the "bet" on what might happen with the stock price. This value is influenced by things like volatility, time decay, and interest rates. By the time an option expires, its extrinsic value will always be zero, no matter what.

Intrinsic Value

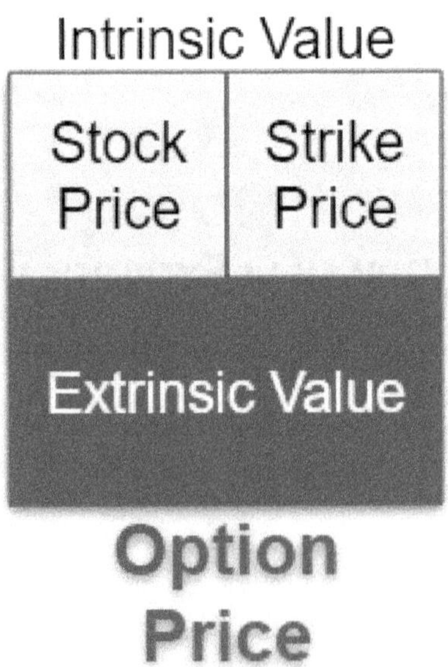

Intrinsic value is easy to calculate. It's just the difference between the current stock price and the strike price, but only when that difference works in favor of the option holder. For a call option, intrinsic value is the amount the stock price is above the strike price. For a put option, it's the amount the stock price is below the strike price. If the difference is negative, the intrinsic value is zero because why would you buy higher or sell lower than the market price?

For example, if you hold a $50 strike call on a stock trading at $55, the intrinsic value of your option is $5. This is the profit you'd theoretically make if you exercised the option, bought the shares at $50, and sold them at the current market price of $55. It's a simple calculation but an important one to understand the real, immediate value of your option.

Extrinsic Value

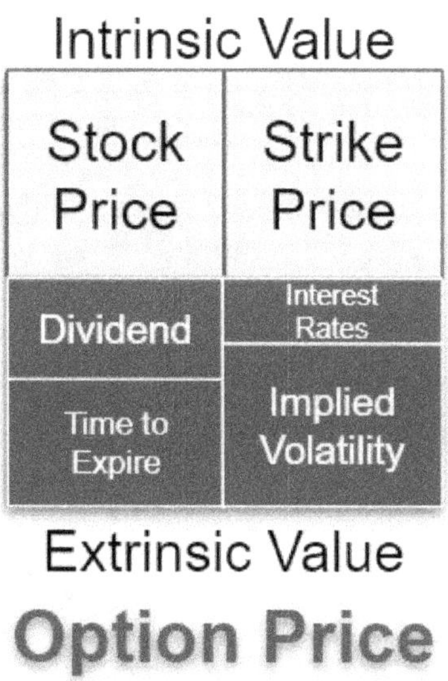

Extrinsic value is a bit more complicated. Every option has extrinsic value until it expires, and when the option expires, the only value left is intrinsic. If there's no intrinsic value, the option expires worthless. Extrinsic value takes into account several other factors that affect an option's price, including:

- **Time Decay:** Options lose value as they get closer to expiration. This is known as time decay. The more time until expiration, the more extrinsic value an option has because there's more time for the stock to move in a favorable direction.
- **Volatility:** This measures how much the stock price is expected to fluctuate. Higher volatility means higher extrinsic value because there's a greater chance the stock price will move enough to make the option profitable.
- **Interest Rates:** While not a major factor, interest rates can still play a role. Higher rates can increase the extrinsic value of call options since the cost of directly buying the stock is higher, making the option more attractive.

Calculating extrinsic value is about understanding how these factors interact with market conditions and the specifics of the option contract.

Out-of-the-money options are all extrinsic value. In-the-money options are a mix of intrinsic and extrinsic value.

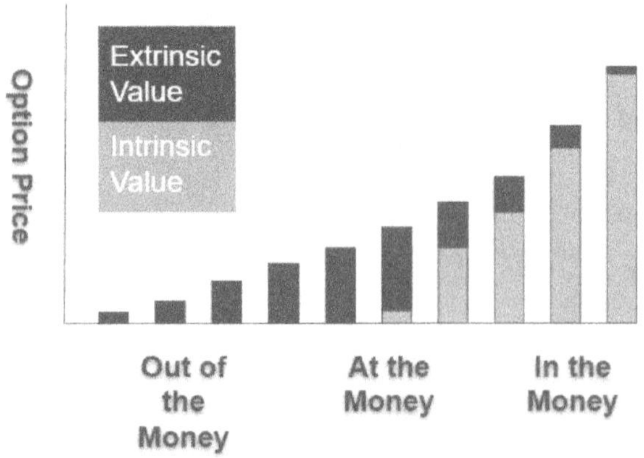

Extrinsic value is highest for at-the-money (ATM) options, where the strike price is right around the current stock price. ATM options are valuable because they sit on the edge of uncertainty; there's a good chance they could end up in the money with just a small move in the stock price. That potential for a quick flip makes them attractive to traders, which is why they carry more extrinsic value.

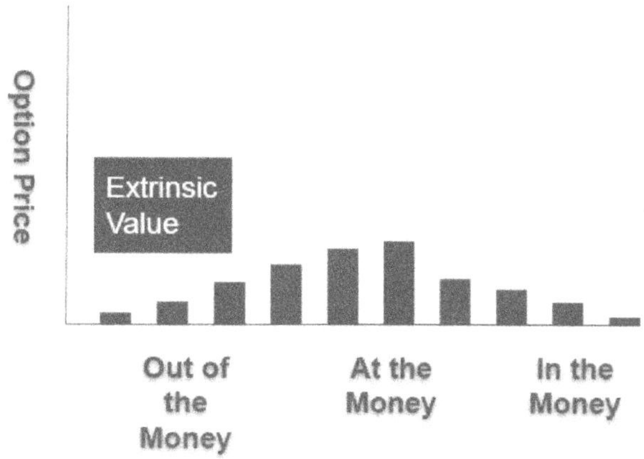

ATM options are also more sensitive to changes in implied volatility. If volatility increases, it boosts the extrinsic value of ATM options more than it does for in-the-money or out-of-the-money options. This makes ATM options particularly valuable when the market is volatile.

As options approach expiration, all options lose extrinsic value, but ATM options lose it the fastest. As time runs out, the uncertainty about the stock's direction fades, and that causes the extrinsic value to drop quickly. This rapid time decay is a result of the high extrinsic value built into these options.

3.5 Test Your Knowledge

You've learned a lot about options, so let's see how much has stuck. These questions aren't just about recalling facts, they're here to help you put what you've learned to use in real-life scenarios.

- If a stock is trading at $52 and you hold a long call with a strike price of $45, what's the intrinsic value of your option?
- Let's say you expect a stock's price to jump. What long or short options could you use to take advantage of this movement?
- How does time decay affect your strategy when choosing between short-term and long-term options?
- Why might someone sell a put option, and what risks would they face?
- How can options be used as a hedge in a diversified portfolio?
- What happens if you exercise an option early, and when might it make sense to do so?

These questions are meant to deepen your understanding and help you start thinking like an experienced trader, weighing different situations and coming up with solid strategies.

Practical Application

To help connect theory to real-world practice, here are three exercises you can try to build your skills in options trading:

1. **Market Analysis Exercise:** Pick a stock and follow its price movements and any related news for a week. Based on what you observe, decide whether you'd buy a call or a put option. Choose a strike price and expiration date, and explain why you made those choices based on what's happening with the stock. Then, track the option for a week. Would your trade have made money?

2. **Options Pricing Exercise:** Select three different stocks and calculate the price of a call and a put option for each, using different strike prices. Look at how changes in the stock price, volatility, and time to expiration affect the option prices.

3. **Trading Simulation:** Try out virtual trading using an online stock market simulator or even a spreadsheet. Practice buying and selling calls and puts. Keep track of your results and think about which strategies worked best in different market conditions. This hands-on experience will be a big help when you start trading for real, especially when you begin combining options to create spreads.

By working through these exercises, you'll reinforce what you've learned and get practical experience that will be essential when you start trading in real markets. The goal here is to blend learning with doing, which is the key to turning knowledge into skills you can actually use.

CHAPTER 4

DIVE DEEP INTO OPTIONS MECHANICS

IMAGINE STEPPING INTO AN art auction where instead of bidding on the artwork directly, you bet on what someone else will pay for that artwork in the future. You're looking ahead, next week, next month, maybe even next year, trying to guess where the value might go. That's kind of like options trading. With options, each work of art is actually an equity.

In an auction house, along with the auctioneer calling out bids, there is also a buzz in the room, rumors, shifting opinions, and everything swirling around.

In order to make an educated assessment, you need the right tools. That's where understanding the Greeks and volatility come in. They help you understand the market better so you can make smarter trades.

4.1 Implied Volatility

Have you noticed how option prices can change, even if the stock doesn't? That's because of implied volatility (IV). IV shows what the market expects in terms of how much the stock's price could move. It doesn't tell you if the stock will go up or down, but it suggests that big moves could happen.

What is Implied Volatility?

IV shows how much price movement the market expects. It plays a big role in pricing options because it helps traders understand how wild the market might get. For example, if a company is about to release earnings or there's big news coming, IV often rises. That's the market getting ready for some major price swings.

It's like planning a trip. If the weather forecast says it'll be calm, you pack light. But if a storm might hit, you bring extra stuff. When IV is high, traders expect big moves and adjust their strategies. This could be because of company news, economic reports, or just general market changes.

Why IV Matters

IV matters because it changes the price of options. When IV is high, option premiums go up. That's because there's a better chance the option could end up in the money (ITM). So if you're buying, you'll pay more. If you're selling, you'll get more because you're taking on more risk.

Implied Volatility vs. Historical Volatility

IV is different from historical volatility (HV). HV looks at how much the stock price has moved in the past, while IV is about what could happen next. HV tells you what's already happened, and IV is about what might happen next.

Tools for Tracking IV

There are tools that can help you track IV. One of the best-known is the VIX, or the "fear gauge." The VIX measures expected volatility for the next 30 days on the S&P 500 (SPX) options. A high VIX means the market expects big swings.

Another tool is IV rank, which compares the current IV to the highs and lows over the past year. When the IV rank is high, volatility is close to the top. When it's low, it's at the bottom. IV rank helps you figure out when to enter or exit trades based on how much action is happening.

Tracking IV can guide your decisions in the options market. Just remember, IV isn't perfect; it's only one part of the bigger picture in your strategy.

4.2 Options Greeks

If you've ever wondered how experienced traders stay so precise in the options market, it's often because they understand the Greeks. These tools help you figure out how options prices might change based on things like stock price moves, time, volatility, and interest rates. Knowing the Greeks is like having a map and compass; it helps you plan your trades based on your expectations, goals, and how much risk you're comfortable taking rather than just hoping for the best.

The Greeks, Delta, Gamma, Theta, Vega, and Rho, each focus on different things that affect an option's price. They help you see both the risks and rewards in any trade. For example, while technical and fundamental analysis tells you what to buy or sell, the Greeks show you how your positions are expected to react as the market moves. This extra layer of insight lets you adjust your trades based on what's happening so you can better manage your risk and increase your chances of making a profit.

If you want to get serious about options trading, understanding the Greeks is a must. They show you how market changes affect your trades and your entire portfolio. By learning how to adjust your positions as things shift, you can trade more confidently and effectively. Let's break down these tools so you can use them to your advantage.

Delta and Gamma: Measuring Speed and Impact

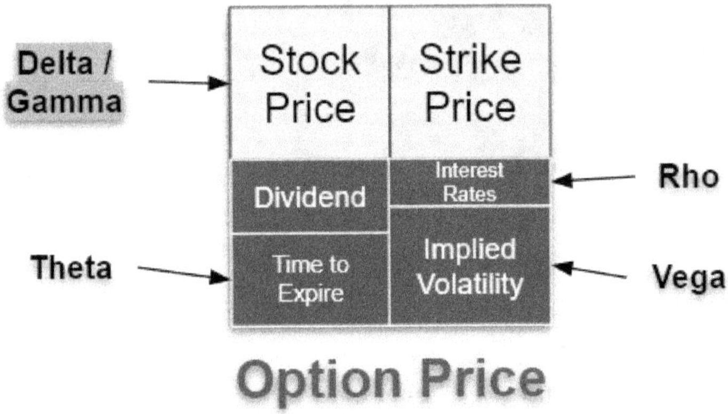

Delta and Gamma are two of the most important Greeks when it comes to tracking how price changes in the underlying stock affect an option. Delta shows how much the option's price will move based on the stock's price changes, while Gamma tells you how fast Delta itself is changing. Think of Delta as your speedometer and Gamma as your acceleration. Getting the hang of these will sharpen your trading skills and help you make quicker, more informed decisions.

Delta: The Rate of Change due to Price Action

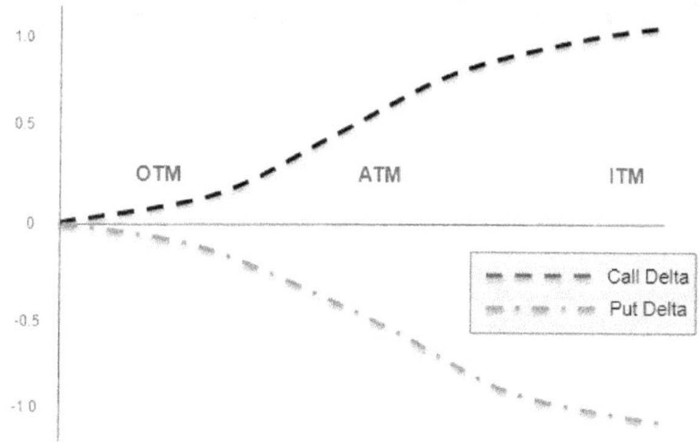

Delta tells you how much the option's price will move when the stock price changes. It's like a sensitivity meter. For long puts, Delta ranges from -1 to 0, and for long calls, it's between 0 and 1. Delta shows how much the option's value will increase or decrease with a $1 move in the underlying stock.

For example, if a long call has a Delta of 0.5, then for every $1 increase in the stock price, the option premium goes up by 50 cents per share ($50 per contract). The opposite is also true: a $1 decrease in the stock price would lower the option's value by 50 cents per share.

Delta doesn't stay the same, it changes throughout the life of the option. But at expiration, every option will end up with a Delta of either -1, 0, or 1.

Long calls and short puts have positive Delta, meaning they gain from bullish moves. Short calls and long puts have negative Delta, meaning they profit from bearish moves. Delta helps you estimate how much profit or loss you can expect if the stock moves in either direction. If you hold a call option on a rising stock and see a high Delta, you can expect that the option's value will increase significantly.

Pro Tip:

None of the other Greeks apply to long stock positions. However, long stock can be thought of as having a Delta of +1 because, for every $1 increase or decrease in stock price, you gain or lose $1 per share. This becomes important when calculating the Net Greeks for positions that combine stock and options as well as when balancing the Net Greeks for your overall portfolio.

Gamma: The Rate of Change in Delta

While Delta tells you how much an option's price will move with the stock price, Gamma measures how quickly Delta itself changes. If Delta is your speedometer, Gamma is your acceleration. Gamma shows how much Delta will change with a $1 move in the stock.

Gamma increases when the stock price is close to the option's strike price (at the money) and decreases when it moves further away from the strike price (in or out of the money). It's highest when the stock trades near the strike price and tends to increase as expiration approaches, especially for at-the-money options.

Let's look at an example. Imagine stock XYZ is trading at $100. You have an at-the-money (ATM) long call option with a Delta of 0.5 and a Gamma of 0.05.

- If XYZ moves up by $1, Delta increases by Gamma multiplied by the $1 move.

    - New Delta = 0.5 + (0.05 * 1) = 0.55

- If XYZ moves down by $1, Delta decreases by Gamma times the -$1 move.

    - New Delta = 0.5 + (0.05 * -1) = 0.45

In this case, a $1 bullish move increases Delta from 0.5 to 0.55, making the option more sensitive to future price moves. A $1 bearish move decreases Delta from 0.5 to 0.45, reducing sensitivity.

High Gamma means Delta changes fast, leading to big swings in value. This can be good if you're ready to manage risk closely, but it also means you'll need to monitor positions more carefully.

Delta as a Measure of Probability

Delta can also give you a rough idea of the chance that an option will end up in the money at expiration. For instance, if an option has a Delta of 0.25, you can think of it as having about a 25% chance of finishing in the money. This adds another layer to Delta's usefulness when evaluating trades.

Theta: Making the Most of Time Decay in Options

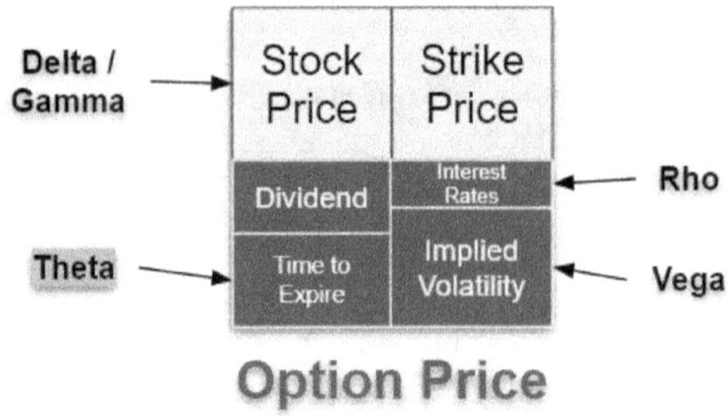

If you've ever watched a clock counting down, you've seen time slipping away. In options trading, Theta works the same way, except instead of time, it's the option's value that gradually fades as the expiration date approaches. Think of it like the shelf life of groceries, just like how milk has an expiration date, so do options, and their value drops the closer they get to that date. This gradual loss in value is what traders call time decay, and it's something you need to understand if you want to get the most out of your trading strategies, especially with credit spreads.

Theta tells you how much the price of an option will drop each day as time passes. It's measured in dollars per day. Theta is negative for long options and positive for short options. So, if Theta is a positive number, it means the position will gain value every day if nothing else changes. If Theta is negative, it means the position will lose value daily. For example, if an option has a Theta of -0.05, that means the price of the option will drop by five cents per share every day, assuming nothing else changes.

While time decay might seem like a bad thing, it's actually something smart traders use to their advantage, especially with short options and credit spreads. The closer an option gets to its expiration date, the faster this time decay kicks in. If the option is out-of-the-money, the price drops even more quickly as time runs out.

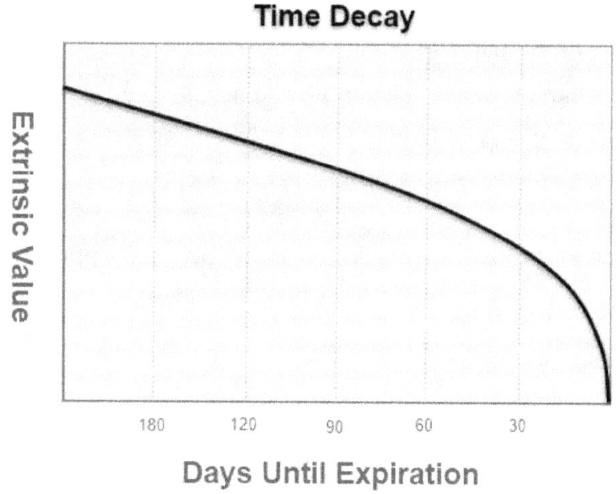

As you approach expiration, time decay speeds up a lot. This can be a problem if you're buying short-term long options, as they can lose value very quickly. Later, when we discuss credit spreads, Theta will become your best friend.

Vega: How Volatility Affects Options

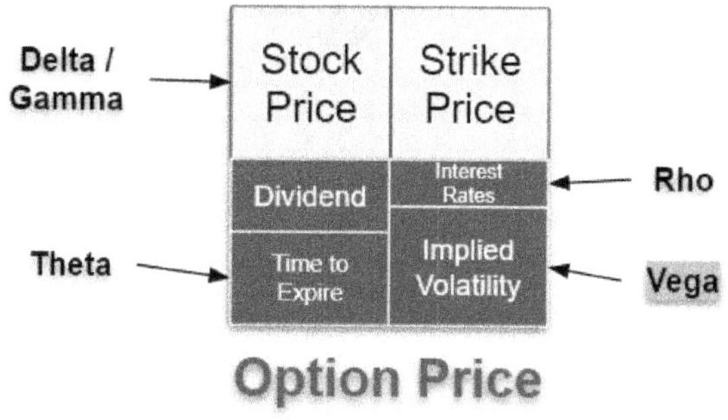

Let's talk about Vega. Vega shows how much an option's price changes based on how volatile the market is. Think of it like a weather vane that tells you how strong the wind (or market volatility) is and how it might push your option's price. Simply put, Vega tells you how much the price of an option could change if implied volatility (IV) moves by 1%.

When the market expects the stock to be more volatile, the price (or premium) of options with longer expirations usually goes up. On the flip side, if the market expects less volatility, the premium drops.

For long options, Vega is positive, and that's usually a good thing. If you buy an option, whether it's a call or a put, you benefit if volatility increases. When volatility goes up, the price of your option goes up, giving you a chance to sell it for more before it expires. For example, if you buy a call and volatility rises due to an earnings report or big news, Vega might push up the price of your call.

For short options, it's the opposite; Vega is negative, and it can work against you. When you sell an option, you get paid upfront, hoping the option will lose value and expire worthless. But if volatility increases, Vega could increase the option's price, and you might have to spend more to buy it back than you got paid. This is a risk, especially with naked options where your losses can get big fast.

Vega is also a good indicator of market sentiment. When uncertainty is high or big events are coming, like earnings reports or economic news, Vega tends to go up as traders expect bigger swings in stock prices. Looking at Vega helps traders understand the risks and rewards of their options and also the mood of the market. A high Vega can mean traders are gearing up for something big.

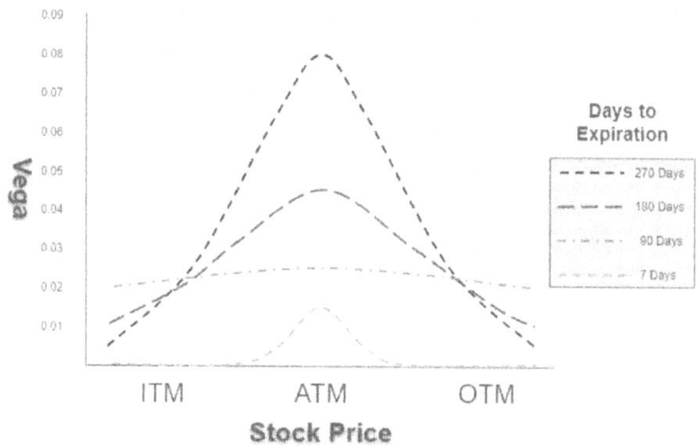

Vega is higher for options with longer expiration dates because there's more time for the stock to experience big price changes. Think of it like planning a road trip. The further away your trip is, the more likely something unexpected, like bad weather, could happen. Similarly, with options, the longer the time to expiration, the more chance for volatility.

Vega is also higher for at-the-money (ATM) options compared to in-the-money (ITM) or out-of-the-money (OTM) options. ATM options are at the tipping point where small changes in the stock's price can make a big difference in whether the option ends up in or out of the money.

For example, if there's news that could cause a major shift in the stock price, like a product launch or a big earnings report, a long-term ATM option's price will reflect a bigger change in volatility expectations compared to short-term or ITM or OTM options. That's because ATM options have more room to swing in either direction, so they're more sensitive to changes in volatility.

This higher Vega can offer some strategic advantages. If you expect volatility to increase but aren't sure which way the stock will move, buying long-term ATM options might be a smart play. Even if the stock doesn't move much, the increase in volatility could boost the option's value and give you a profitable trade.

On the other hand, if you think volatility will drop, selling long-term ATM options might work in your favor. As volatility falls, Vega will push the option's price down, letting you buy it back for less than what you sold it for, locking in a profit.

Most trading platforms show Vega values for different options, helping you compare and choose which ones to trade. Watching general volatility indicators, like the VIX, can also give you clues about where Vega might be headed and help you make smarter trading decisions.

Rho: How Interest Rates Affect Options

Rho is one of the Greeks that measures how much an option's price will change with a one percent move in interest rates. For call options, if interest rates go up, it costs more to hold cash, which makes buying the stock outright less appealing. As a result, call options, which require less upfront cash, might see their prices rise. On the other hand, higher interest rates can lower the value of put options because the potential returns from holding cash start looking better compared to holding a declining asset.

In a low-interest-rate world, it's cheaper to hold on to assets, making long-term investments more attractive. That could lead to less demand for options since traders might prefer buying the stocks directly. But when interest rates are higher, holding stocks becomes more expensive, which can make options, especially long-term ones, a more cost-effective way to benefit from stock price movements without tying up a lot of capital upfront.

Out of all the Greeks, Rho doesn't get as much attention because options are generally less sensitive to changes in interest rates. It's the least impactful compared to factors like Delta or Vega, so traders don't rely on it as much.

Think of Rho as a tool that shows how much your option might react to changes in interest rates. However, keep in mind that interest rates reflect the bigger picture of economic policy. Central banks raise or lower rates to either give the economy a boost or cool it down. These changes can ripple through the stock market and impact options prices along the way.

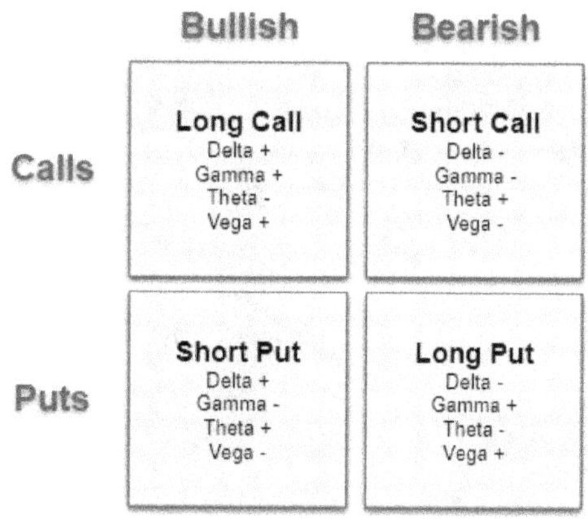

4.3 COMBINING THE GREEKS: BUILDING A SOLID STRATEGY

ONCE YOU MOVE BEYOND just buying and selling single options, you can start combining them to build strategies that match what's happening in the market. Think of it as leading a band where each Greek, Delta, Gamma, Theta, and Vega has its part to play. Your job is to make sure they work together to help boost your profits.

As the bandleader, you decide how each piece fits into the overall performance. Delta, Gamma, Theta, and Vega all bring something different to the table, and it's up to you to find the right balance. When you get it right, your strategy becomes more stable and predictable. By understanding how to tweak the Greeks, you can create trades that align with your market outlook while keeping your risk in check.

To know how your strategy will hold up in the market, you'll need to calculate your Net Greeks, Delta, Gamma, Theta, and Vega based on the types of options and the number of contracts you're using.

Calculating Net Greeks

Here's a simple example to show you how it works. Let's say you're expecting a stock to go up over the next few days. You buy 5 long call options 30 days from expiration:

- **5 ATM long calls:** Delta 0.50, Theta -24.29

To find your Net Position Delta (NPD), you multiply the Delta by the number of contracts:(5 * 0.5) = 2.50 NPD. This means your portfolio would gain $250 for every $1 increase in the stock price.

To find your Net Position Theta (NPT), you do the same with the Theta:(5 * -24.29) = -121.45 NPT. This means your options would lose $121.45 of value each day that the trade remains open.

> **Pro Tip:** Delta is usually shown as a per-share value, but some brokers display Theta as a per-contract value. Make sure you know which your broker is using.

With these numbers, you can estimate how profitable your trade could be based on the stock's expected movement over time. For instance, if the stock goes up by $1 over the next two days, you can calculate the potential profit or loss like this:

- **Formula:** (NPD * 100 * Price change) - (NPT * Days open)
- **Calculation:** (2.50 * 100 * $1) - (121.45 * 2) = $250 - $242.90 = $7.10 profit

What can you do in this situation? You could hope for a bigger bullish move, but hope isn't a strategy. A better idea might be to add options with positive Theta to reduce your risk in case the stock only moves sideways or slightly up.

Let's add 5 OTM short calls to see how it changes the trade. Now your position looks like this:

- **5 ATM long calls:** Delta 0.50, Theta -24.29
- **5 OTM short calls:** Delta -0.35, Theta +19.70

Selling the short calls reduced your cost to enter the trade by over 50%!

Pro Tip: Greeks are shown from a long-position perspective. So, when calculating short options, reverse the Greeks. For example, a short call has a negative Delta because it shows how much the option price could drop with a $1 bullish move.

Now, let's recalculate:

- **New NPD:** (5 * 0.5) + (5 * -0.35) = 0.75 NPD. This means your portfolio would gain $75 for every $1 increase in the stock price.
- **New NPT:** (5 * -24.29) + (5 * 19.70) = -22.95 NPT. This means your

options would lose $22.95 of value each day the trade remains open.

Your NPD went down, meaning your trade won't gain as much from a bullish move as before. But your NPT also went down, meaning time decay won't hurt you as much, either. Let's see how the new strategy performs with a $1 move in two days:

- **Formula:** (NPD * 100 * Price change) - (NPT * Days open)
- **Calculation:** (0.75 * 100 * $1) + (-22.95 * 2) = $75 - $45.90 = $29.10 profit

By lowering your Theta loss, you turned a small $7 profit into $29.10 while also reducing your risk by over 50%. Lower Theta means your trade can become profitable faster, even with a smaller price move.

Balancing the Greeks is key to avoiding situations where one position hurts you more than another helps.

Pro Tip: This calculation gives an estimate of your profit or loss, but it won't be exact since Greek values change as the market moves.

Whenever you set up trades with multiple options, it helps to calculate the Net Greeks of your position. This is especially important when building spreads or combining long and short positions.

For example, if you expect market volatility to rise, you might want to increase your Net Vega. Or, if you think the market will settle down, you could adjust your trade so that Theta plays a bigger role.

Real-World Example

Here's a real-life example. In May 2023, a trader used a combination of Greeks to profit from a volatile market. They set up a long strangle on SPY, which tracks the S&P 500. A strangle involves buying both a call and a put option with the same expiration date but at different strike prices. At first, this is a Delta-neutral trade because the positive Delta from the call cancels out the negative Delta from the put. But as soon as the stock moves, Gamma starts to push the Delta in favor of the winning side.

The trader used this strategy because they expected volatility to increase over the next few days. As volatility rose, Vega caused both options to go up in value, and the trader was able to close the trade for a 28% profit in just 24 hours.

By carefully balancing the Greeks, they maximized profits while minimizing the risk of a bad price move.

This kind of approach, where you look at different factors and opportunities, is what separates successful option traders from the rest. By getting comfortable with the Greeks and learning how to mix them together, you can create strategies that don't just follow the market but aim for profit no matter which way it moves. With this level of planning, options trading becomes less of a gamble and more of a smart, calculated part of your investment game plan.

4.4 Test Your Knowledge

Now that you've got a good grasp of the material, it's time to see how well you can apply it. These questions are meant to help you think through the concepts in real trading situations, not just recall facts. The goal is to test your understanding and see how ready you are to use these ideas in the market.

- If an option has a high Vega and market volatility suddenly spikes, what will likely happen to the option's price?
- What could happen to your options strategy if the Delta of your key holdings suddenly increases?
- Below are the Net Greeks for a trade (with names and strike prices removed).

Net Position Delta: +.30
Net Position Gamma: -.05
Net Position Theta: +2.25
Net Position Vega: -.15

- Based on these values, answer the following:
    - What trend is this trade positioned for: bullish, bearish, or neither?

  - Would this strategy benefit from a rise in IV or be hurt by it?
  - Will this trade make money over time or lose value because of time decay?

- Describe a scenario where adjusting the Greeks in your portfolio could help reduce risk during a period of high volatility.
- How would you interpret a situation where an asset's historical volatility is much lower than its implied volatility? What action might you take?
- What could you do if an option you hold has rising Vega, but the underlying stock's price is dropping?

Practical Application

To really get the hang of these concepts, practice is key. Here are three exercises to help you bring what you've learned into real-world situations:

1. **Monitor and Analyze Volatility:** Track a stock with upcoming earnings and follow the implied volatility of three different options with the same strike price but different expiration dates. Watch how the IV changes before and after earnings, and note which option was most impacted. Think about how you could use that information to build an options strategy.
2. **Build a Greek-Focused Portfolio:** Set up a virtual portfolio with a mix of options and try to balance the Greeks. Over a month, tweak your portfolio as the market shifts, and see how your understanding

of the Greeks improves your decisions.

3. **Simulate Interest Rate Changes:** Using an options pricing model, play out what happens if interest rates rise or fall by 1%. Look at how Rho influences your options and think about adjustments you could make to shield your portfolio or take advantage of these changes.

Doing these exercises gives you hands-on experience and helps you get a better feel for making choices and fine-tuning your strategies. The more you practice, the easier it'll be to tackle the challenges that come with real trading.

Chapter 5

Introduction to Credit Spreads

So far, we've covered how to pick stocks for your watchlist and how to use a mix of fundamental, technical, and sentimental analysis to form expectations for those stocks. You've also learned how individual options work, how to calculate risk and reward, and how the Greeks come into play when you're dealing with multiple options. Now it's time to pull it all together and dive into spread trades. This is where you'll see how combining options can open up new opportunities that go beyond just trading single options.

Credit spreads are a great example of how pairing multiple options can improve your trading. Using a mix of options lets you set up trades that can take advantage of market movements while keeping your risk under control. The great thing about these strategies is that you can adjust them based on your own risk comfort, how you think the market will move, and what you want to achieve financially.

In this chapter, we'll break down how credit spreads work and why they're such a valuable tool to have in your trading strategy.

5.1 What is a Credit Spread?

Definition and Mechanics

When you see the word "spread" in the name of an options strategy, it means you're dealing with multiple options of the same type, like long calls paired with short calls or long puts with short puts. And when you see "credit," it tells you that the main action involves short options, where you're making money by collecting premiums. A "credit spread," therefore, is a trade where short options are the primary instruments and long options are used to limit your risk.

The key here is that the options you sell are more expensive than the ones you buy, which creates a net credit. That credit is your potential profit.

This lets you generate income while giving you the flexibility to control your risk.

Risk and Reward

The goal is to find the right balance between risk and reward for you. As Warren Buffett famously said, "It's only when the tide goes out that you know who's been swimming naked." In trading, naked options are those without any protection, and when the market turns, traders using these options are often hit the hardest. Credit spreads provide a safer way to trade by allowing you to limit your risk.

When investing in stocks, you calculate your return based on the difference between what you paid for your shares and what you can sell them for. To evaluate your performance, you calculate your Return on Investment (ROI) by dividing your profit by the initial amount spent on the stock. For example, if you bought 100 shares of Apple (AAPL) at $180 each and later sold them at $190, your profit would be $10 per share. Dividing this profit by the $180 you initially spent gives you an ROI of approximately 5.5%.

However, with credit spreads, the calculation is different. Since you are being paid to enter the trade, there's no upfront investment cost to use for calculating ROI. Your maximum profit comes from the difference between the premiums collected from selling short options and what you pay for the long options. Your maximum risk is the difference between the strike prices of the short and long options minus the net premium received. To calculate your return on a credit spread, you should look at your Return on Risk (ROR), which is your maximum profit divided by your maximum risk.

Let's break this down with an example. If you sell a $180 call on AAPL for $4.40 per share and buy a $190 call for $0.92 per share, both expiring at the same time, your net credit and potential profit would be $3.48 per share or $348 per contract. If the market moves against you, your maximum loss is capped at the difference between the strike prices ($10), minus the $3.48 credit. This leaves you with a risk of $6.52 per share or $652 per contract. Therefore, your Return on Risk (ROR) for this trade would be approximately 53.4%.

Income Generation through Premiums

When you set up a credit spread, you receive an upfront payment by collecting a premium from the options you sell. This potential for generating a regular income stream makes credit spreads particularly attractive to traders looking to supplement their earnings or replace their existing income. Unlike other trading strategies, credit spreads have a defined maximum risk, which enables traders to clearly understand their potential losses. As a result, this structure provides a safety net against significant market downturns, allowing you to trade with greater confidence and peace of mind.

5.2 Selecting the Right Stocks and Strikes for Spreads

When setting up a credit spread, the first step is to identify a stock with strong financials and steady growth. Stocks that exhibit these qualities tend to behave more predictably, making them easier to trade. Additionally, focus on stocks that have high trading volume for both shares and options. This ensures that you can enter and exit trades smoothly. Having good liquidity helps maintain efficiency when making trades.

Volatility is also an important factor to consider. Higher volatility can lead to higher premiums, but it also introduces more risk, so it's crucial to find the right balance.

Selecting the appropriate strike prices is crucial. It's essential to balance potential risk and reward. One common mistake among newer traders is choosing strike prices that are too far out of the money. While this may increase the likelihood that the options will expire worthless, something you want for a credit spread, these far out-of-the-money options offer significantly smaller premiums. Which means you end up taking on significant risk for a comparatively low reward.

A more effective strategy is to utilize technical analysis to identify stocks that are trending in distinct patterns. Pay attention to support and resistance levels, as they can assist you in determining the best strike prices to maximize your return while also having good odds of expiring worthless. Additionally, review the company's fundamentals to ensure it is financially stable, helping you avoid surprises from unexpected news or earnings reports.

When it comes to trading options, timing is really important! As time goes on, options gradually lose value, and this is known as theta decay. If you're selling options, this decay can actually work in your favor. Just keep in mind that the closer you get to the expiration date, the faster options will lose their value.

Some new traders might be tempted to sell very short-term options because they do decrease in value quickly. However, this strategy can backfire since most of the extrinsic value might already be gone, leaving you with more risk for only a tiny potential reward.

On the flip side, longer-term options can offer greater gains. But if you pick an expiration date that's too far away, the theta decay will be slow, which means you'll have to wait longer to see any profits. The upside is that this gives you extra time to adjust if the market changes.

To find a sweet spot, it's best to choose an expiration date that still has some good premium left but is also close enough for the value to drop quickly. Aiming for options that expire in about 30 days is often a great middle ground. This way, you can capture a decent amount of premium while still benefiting from faster decay and potential profits in a reasonable timeframe.

Figuring out when to close your trade is an important and sometimes tricky decision. You might be tempted to hang on until the very last moment to try to squeeze out every bit of profit, but locking in a decent gain early on can actually lower your risk and give you some extra cash for other trades. Keep in mind that as expiration gets closer, option prices can swing unpredictably, which is known as gamma risk. So, closing early can be a smart choice, especially if you're dealing with at-the-money options.

In the end, setting up credit spreads is all about bringing together the right elements: picking the stock, choosing the appropriate strike prices, and timing your trades just right. Don't feel rushed! If a trade doesn't look perfect, it's completely okay to wait for a better opportunity. With experience, you'll start to recognize solid setups and fine-tune your trades more easily.

5.3 How Wide Should I Make My Spreads?

The difference between the strike prices of the options you're selling and the ones you're buying is an important factor you can tweak to make your credit spread trade more aggressive or more conservative. A wider spread can lead to bigger rewards, but it also means taking on greater risks.

A wider spread can mean a bigger premium in your pocket because you don't need to invest as much in the long option since it's further out of the money. But there's a catch: the larger the gap between your strike prices means the short option can move further against you before your long option steps in to help.

As you decide how wide to set your spreads, keep a few important things in mind. First, think about your personal risk tolerance. Do you find yourself checking the stock ticker all day, or do you prefer to take a step back and look at your trades once a week with a clear head? Your comfort level with risk will be a big factor in how wide you want to go. If you lean towards a conservative approach, narrower spreads might be more your style; they provide more security, even if the returns are smaller. But if you're up for taking on a little more risk for the chance at a bigger payout, you could structure your trades using wider spreads.

Market volatility can influence the width you feel comfortable using for your spread trades. When the market experiences significant fluctuations, prices can change rapidly, which can have both positive and negative effects on your trades. In such situations, opting for narrower spreads can help protect you from substantial losses, as they are less affected by sharp price movements. Conversely, in a more stable market, wider spreads can enable you to earn more since the likelihood of prices moving against you is lower.

Then, there is position sizing within your portfolio. How much of your capital do you feel comfortable investing in a single trade? Finding the right position size is essential to make sure you're not too exposed in any one trade, which helps keep your portfolio safe from significant hits. As a general rule, wider spreads work better for larger positions, while narrower spreads might be a better fit for smaller ones.

5.4 Test Your Knowledge

Now that you have covered the key concepts, it's time to test your knowledge. These questions will help reinforce and deepen your understanding of credit spread trading:

- When setting up a credit spread, which option is typically closer to the at-the-money (ATM) price: the short option or the long option?
- Why might a trader choose credit spreads over selling naked options?
- How can a trader calculate the maximum possible loss on a credit spread?
- What should a trader consider when deciding whether to close a credit spread position early?
- How does selecting a shorter expiration date affect the risk and potential return of a credit spread compared to a longer expiration date?
- How does rising market volatility impact the premiums on the options in a credit spread?

Practical Application

To turn theory into practice, here are three hands-on exercises designed to strengthen your skills in setting up and managing credit spreads. These activities will help you apply what you've learned in a safe, controlled environment before implementing your strategies in the real market.

1. **Diminishing Returns Exercise:** Choose a stock and observe the bid and ask prices for both call and put options. Notice how quickly the option values decrease as the strike prices move further from the at-the-money price. At what point does a spread trade become unfeasible, such that the bid price of the higher strike option equals the ask price of the lower strike? Compare the values of options at the same strike price but with different expiration dates. Take note of how both time and strike price affect the option premiums.

2. **Market Analysis Diary:** For one week, track three stocks by recording their daily closing prices, volatility levels, and any major news events that impact them. Analyze the trends you observe. Are all three stocks moving in the same direction? If you were to place a credit spread based on your analysis, would you use the same type of spread for all three (bullish, bearish, or range-bound)? Document your thought process and decisions in a diary format, which will sharpen your ability to analyze market trends and match them to appropriate options strategies.

3. **Technical Analysis Practice:** Select three stocks and analyze their historical price movements. Identify key support and resistance levels based on their behavior over the past several months. Then, monitor

these stocks for a month to see if the support and resistance levels hold. If they don't, try to determine the causes. Was it due to earnings reports, economic news, or other factors? This exercise will provide you with deeper insights into how these levels can be influenced by external events and help you anticipate price movements more effectively.

CHAPTER 6

BULL PUT SPREADS

STRATEGIES FOR A RISING MARKET

IMAGINE A STRATEGY THAT empowers you to profit when the market rises, remains steady, or even dips slightly. It may sound incredible, but it's entirely achievable with bull put spreads! This method is ideal for those who believe in a stock's potential while also wanting to safeguard their investments. Consider bull put spreads as a means to harness the power of stable or growing markets while providing a layer of protection.

In Chapter 3, we ventured into long and short puts. Now, we'll combine these concepts into a robust strategy that can elevate your trading experience. Selling short puts allows you to earn income by agreeing to buy 100 shares of a stock at a designated price for an upfront payment. Yet, for traders with smaller portfolios, the capital needed can be daunting. It's understandable to feel frustrated when faced with the challenge of selling options on lower-priced stocks that yield minimal premium, all while trying to avoid risking too much of your hard-earned capital. Trading on margin can add an extra layer of stress, leading to uncomfortable situations when margin calls come into play.

Naked puts can leave you vulnerable, potentially requiring you to purchase 100 shares of a declining stock, leaving you waiting for a hoped-for recovery. And in the worst-case scenario, the stock might fall to zero, yielding a complete loss.

However, this is precisely where bull put spreads shine! They enable you to engage with high-quality stocks while only risking a fraction of the capital needed for naked puts. By embracing bull put spreads, you can pursue the same or even greater income potential while maintaining a strong grip on your risk.

Let's meet Jane. Her friend Steve introduced her to options trading. He had been generating income each month by selling naked puts. In June, when XYZ stock was trading at $122.65, Steve sold a $113 strike put that was set to expire one month later and collected $1.71 per share, totaling $171 per contract. This gave him a Return on Risk (ROR) of 1.5%. His trade tied up $11,300 in risk capital because if XYZ's price fell, he would be obligated to buy 100 shares at $113 each.

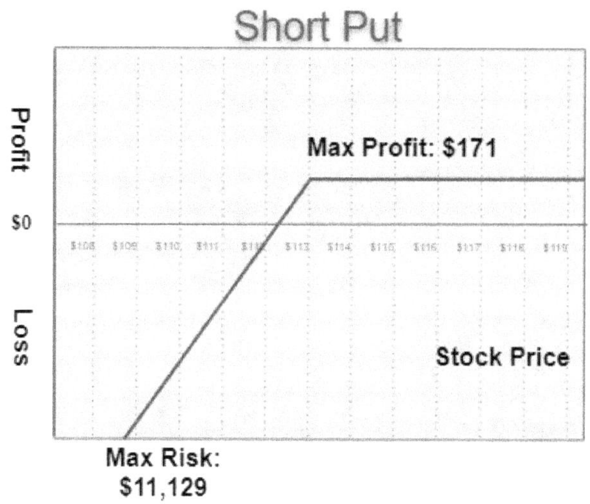

Jane had a modest portfolio, which meant that selling just one put option would use up most of her capital. While trading on margin was a possibility, it came with the risk of big losses if the stock price dropped, and Jane didn't feel comfortable risking more than what she had in her account.

That's when she stumbled upon bull put spreads! This strategy was a game changer for her, allowing her to earn some income while keeping her risk in check. With bull put spreads, Jane could trade the same valuable stocks and enjoy higher premiums without tying up all her cash. This approach gave her better income potential compared to selling naked puts but with much less risk.

In the sections ahead, we'll dive into how bull put spreads work, share some practical examples, and guide you on how to make this strategy part of your trading repertoire. By the end of it, you'll be all set to add bull put spreads to your toolkit and make more informed, profitable decisions in the market. Let's jump in and get started!

6.1 Bull Put Structure

A BULL PUT SPREAD is an options trading strategy that involves selling a put option to collect the premium and using part of that premium to buy a long put option at a lower strike price, both with the same expiration date. The long put serves as a hedge, helping to limit your risk. You can achieve maximum profit as long as the stock price remains above the strike price of the short put at expiration, which allows for potential profits in various scenarios.

Setting up a bull put spread is relatively straightforward. First, identify a stock that you believe will either maintain its price or increase. Next, look for support levels—price points where the stock tends to stabilize and rebound. Set the strike price of your short put at or below this support level. Decide how wide you want your spread to be and select the appropriate strike price for your long put since the width of your spread will determine your maximum risk for the trade. Ensure both options have the same expiration date.

6.2 Calculating Profits

Let's revisit Jane and her friend Steve and their trades on XYZ stock. Jane was bullish on XYZ and wanted to sell puts, but unlike Steve, she wasn't comfortable risking over $11,000 to make just $171. Instead, she decided to use bull put spreads to take advantage of the trend.

Jane sold four puts with a strike price of $113 for $1.71 per share and simultaneously bought four puts with a strike price of $110 for $1.14 per share. Her maximum profit is calculated by finding the difference between the credit received from the short puts ($1.71) and the debit paid for the long puts ($1.14). This difference is then multiplied by 100 (since each contract controls 100 shares) and by the number of contracts (4).

Here's the breakdown: Short put credit ($1.71) - Long put debit ($1.14) = Profit per share. $1.71 - $1.14 = $0.55

Since each contract controls 100 shares, Jane makes $55 per contract. With four contracts, her maximum profit is $220.

Bull Put Profit

Short Put Credit - Long Put Debit = **Net Credit**

Net Credit * Total Contracts = **Max Profit**

As long as XYZ stays above $113, all options will expire worthless, allowing both Jane and Steve to walk away with profitable trades. However, Jane's bull put spreads are earning her 28% more than Steve's naked put!

6.3 Calculating Risks

Not all trades go as planned, so it's essential to understand the rights and obligations associated with each instrument you use in order to accurately assess your risks. While Jane may be earning more money than Steve, we need to examine how much capital she is risking before we can label her trade as a wise decision.

Bull Put Risk

Short Put Strike - Long Put Strike = **Spread**

(Spread - Net Credit) * Total Contracts = **Max Risk**

Each short put option carries the potential obligation to buy 100 shares, while each long put gives the holder the right to sell 100 shares. In Jane's case, she has traded four short puts, meaning she could be obligated to buy 400 shares at $113 each. However, this doesn't mean she is risking $45,200. Her long puts allow her to sell those 400 shares at $110 each.

If the stock price of XYZ were to drop significantly, and Jane was required to buy shares at $113, she could exercise her long puts and sell those shares immediately for $110 each. No matter how much the stock price falls, Jane's maximum loss is capped at $3 per share. Additionally, the premium she received when she initiated the trade reduces her maximum risk to just $2.45 per share. Therefore, Jane's total risk is only $980. Since her broker understands that her risk is defined, they will only require her to set aside enough capital to cover that maximum loss.

So, who has the better trade? Steve has a maximum profit of $171 based on a risk of $11,129, resulting in a return on risk (ROR) of 1.5%. In contrast, Jane has a maximum profit of $220 with a risk of $980, leading to a significantly higher return on risk of 22.4%.

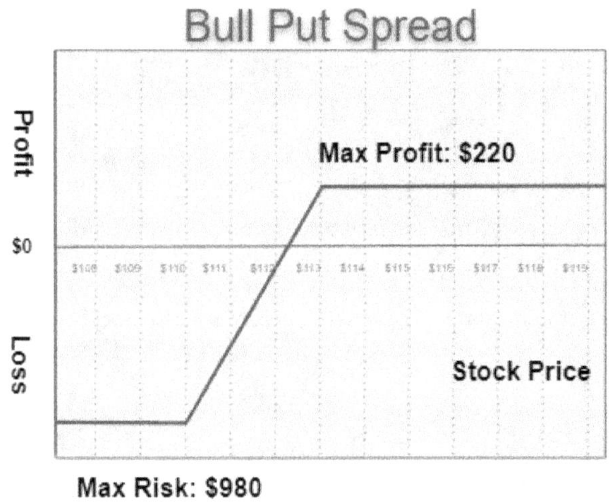

Both trades aim to benefit from the same trend and have similar probabilities of success. However, Jane managed to combine options effectively, reducing her risk by over 90% while increasing her maximum return.

Now, consider what would happen if XYZ's stock plummeted. If XYZ lost a significant contract and its stock price dropped to $60, Steve would be assigned 100 shares at $113. This would result in $11,300 being deducted from his account, leaving him with shares valued at only $6,000. He would incur a loss of $5,300, with the possibility of further losses if the shares continue to decline. If Steve aims for a target return of 1.5% for each trade, this single downturn would wipe out all the profits from his last 30 winning trades. Assuming he is trading monthly options, this loss would erase 2.5 years of profits.

On the other hand, Jane would also face a loss, but hers is capped at $980, regardless of how far the stock falls.

Pro Tip: *What happens if my short-put is assigned early?* Don't worry; your risk is still protected by the long puts. If you are assigned early, your broker can automatically exercise the long put to close out the trade, or if you have the capital, you can choose to accept the assignment and use the long put to safeguard against further bearish moves. As long as the long puts are active, your maximum risk will not exceed the difference between the spread minus the credit you received.

6.4 Bull Put Probability Calculations

Why would anyone take the risk of making a trade where the potential losses are higher than the potential profits, and a single loss could wipe out the gains from multiple winning trades? The answer lies in probability. In options trading, you must find a balance between potential profits, risk, and probability that works for you.

Think of these three aspects as the sides of a triangle. When you change one side, the others get affected, too. If you tweak a trade that impacts profit, risk, or probability, you'll see changes in the other areas as well. For example, let's say you have a strategy that relies on a stock making a specific move. If you adjust it to create a position that can profit from different outcomes at the same time, you'll increase the chances of success, but keep in mind that this will also bring in more risk and reduced rewards.

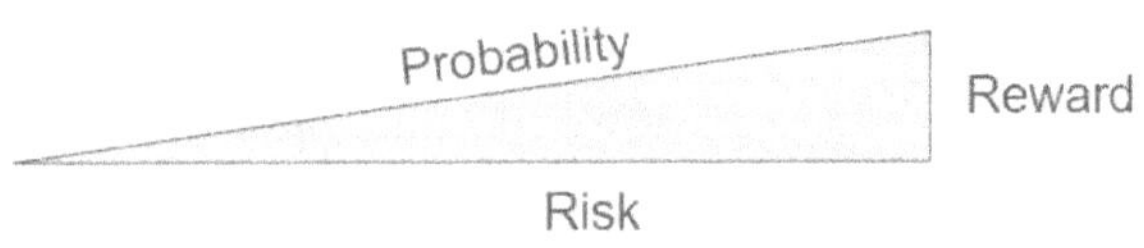

Let's examine how this applies to Bull Put spreads by analyzing two trades that are essentially identical, except for the strike prices used.

Example:

Stock price: $545.34

Both trades involve a 5-point spread and expire in 30 days.

Trade #1: ITM Bull Put

- **Short Put Strike:** $555, Bid: $10.47, Delta: .75
- **Long Put Strike:** $550, Ask: $7.59, Delta: -.59
- **Max profit:** $2.88/share

- **Max risk:** $2.12/share

Trade #2: OTM Bull Put

- **Short Put Strike:** $535, Bid: $2.62, Delta: .24
- **Long Put Strike:** $530, Ask: $1.90, Delta: -.18
- **Max profit:** $0.72/share
- **Max risk:** $4.28/share

Both trades involve a short put option that is approximately $10 away from the stock's current price.

Trade #1 offers a higher maximum profit of $2.88 per share and a lower maximum risk of just $2.12 per share. However, since this trade is in-the-money (ITM), the stock must rise above $555 by the expiration date for you to realize the full profit. If the stock remains flat or declines, this trade could incur losses.

Trade #2 is out-of-the-money (OTM), which means that the stock price can rise, stay the same, or even drop slightly without necessarily leading to a loss. For this trade to be profitable, the stock only needs to remain above $535. As a result, this trade has a smaller maximum profit of $0.72 per share and comes with a higher maximum risk of $4.28 per share. However, because it is OTM and can potentially profit from multiple market directions, this trade has a significantly greater probability of success.

When estimating the chances of success using delta, we find that Trade #1's short put has a delta of 0.75. This indicates a 25% chance of reaching maximum profit. In contrast, Trade #2's short put has a delta of 0.24, which suggests a 76% chance of achieving maximum profit.

Although Trade #1 presents a higher potential reward with lower apparent risk, its lower probability of success makes it the riskier position. Trade #2 offers a greater likelihood of success, but the trade-off is a smaller potential profit and higher risk.

6.5 Bull Put Greeks

Let's analyze the Greeks to understand their impact on a bull put spread, how this strategy generates profit, and the potential challenges it may face.

We'll use the Greeks from Trade #2 as an example:

- Short Put Strike: $535, Bid: $2.62, Delta: .24, Gamma: -.02, Theta: .08, Vega: -.49
- Long Put Strike: $530, Ask: $1.90, Delta: -.18, Gamma: .01, Theta: -.07, Vega: .41

To calculate the Net Greeks, we combine the Greek values of both the short and long options and then multiply them by the number of contracts. For simplicity, we will focus on just one contract.

- **Net Position Delta**: Short Put Delta: .24 + Long Put Delta: -.18 = .06
- **Net Position Gamma**: Short Put Gamma: -.02 + Long Put Gamma: .01 = -.01
- **Net Position Theta**: Short Put Theta: .08 + Long Put Theta: -.07 = .01
- **Net Position Vega**: Short Put Vega: -.49 + Long Put Vega: .41 = -.08

To convert these to per-contract values (instead of per share), we multiply each by 100:

- **Net Position Delta**: 6
- **Net Position Gamma**: -1
- **Net Position Theta**: 1
- **Net Position Vega**: -8

Here's what these Greeks indicate:

- **Delta** is positive, meaning the position benefits when the stock price rises and loses value if the stock price declines.
- **Gamma** is negative, which means that as the stock price increases, Delta decreases. Conversely, if the stock price drops, Delta increases. In other words, the bullish impact on your position diminishes as the stock moves further out-of-the-money (OTM); however, if the stock price starts to fall, the negative effect becomes more pronounced.
- **Theta** is positive because the short put is the main component of the trade. All else being equal, this trade gains value over time as time decay works in your favor.
- **Vega** is negative, indicating that the trade will lose value if implied volatility increases but will benefit if volatility decreases.

Understanding these Greeks provides insight into how the trade will react to different market conditions, allowing for better management of your position.

6.6 When to Use Bull Put Spreads

Understanding when to use a bull put spread can significantly impact your trading success. You should be confident that the market is moving in your favor before committing to this strategy.

The ideal time to employ a bull put spread is when the market or a specific stock is trending upward or is not expected to decline. This is where both your fundamental and technical analysis skills come into play.

On the technical side, tools such as moving averages or the MACD (Moving Average Convergence Divergence) can help confirm a bullish trend. When these indicators show an upward trend, it signifies a positive outlook. Coupling this technical confirmation with strong fundamentals, like robust earnings or favorable news in the industry, provides a solid setup for considering a bull put spread.

Selecting the right strike prices and expiration dates involves both strategy and instinct. It's essential to find a balance between risk and reward that aligns with your trading goals.

For example, if you choose strike prices close to the current stock price with a shorter expiration, you can collect higher premiums and potentially secure quicker profits. However, this approach carries greater risk; if the stock dips even slightly, it could fall below your short strike price.

Alternatively, you may opt for strike prices that are further out-of-the-money, ideally below a strong support level, and choose a longer expiration date. This strategy allows the stock more room to move without jeopardizing your trade, but the immediate returns will be smaller.

Lastly, don't hesitate to close your bull put spread before it expires. If the stock moves favorably and the short options lose most of their value, it's wise to lock in your profits early. Additionally, closing the trade frees up your capital for your next opportunity.

6.7 Monitoring and Managing the Trade

Once your bull put spread is established, your goal is to monitor it without becoming overly preoccupied. Instead of constantly watching the market, set up alerts in your trading platform to notify you of significant price movements or news that could impact your stock. You can also utilize technical analysis to ensure the stock is still performing as anticipated. If it starts to approach the strike price of the put you sold, it's time to evaluate your options.

Making adjustments as the market changes is both strategic and instinctive. If the stock is not moving in your favor, but you believe this change is temporary, you might consider rolling the spread down. This involves closing your current position and opening a new one with lower strike prices in the same transaction. Another option is to roll the trade out in time, extending the expiration date, which will give the stock more time to recover.

On the other hand, if the stock is performing better than expected, it may be wise to lock in your gains by closing the trade early. Ultimately, it's all about weighing the potential upside against the risk of holding on too long.

6.8 Test Your Knowledge

Let's evaluate your understanding of bull put spreads with a few quick questions:

- If the stock price increases a week after initiating a bull put spread, what would be a good strategy to manage your position?
- What effect does a sudden drop in implied volatility have on the value of a bull put spread?
- How do you determine the breakeven point in a bull put spread, and what is the formula for calculating it?
- Why is it important to consider earnings report dates when planning a bull put spread?
- How do expiration dates influence the risk and reward of a bull put spread?
- What indicators suggest it may be a good time to close your bull put spread early?

Practical Application

Put Your Knowledge to Work with These Hands-On Exercises:

1. **Market Simulation**: Set up a virtual bull put spread using current market data on a trading platform or a spreadsheet. Choose a stock that you believe will rise or remain stable. Select strike prices that are appropriate for your outlook and choose an expiration date. Track the trade over the course of a week and observe how market fluctuations impact it.

2. **Variations**: Identify a stock that you expect to trend higher. Create three bull put spreads on that stock using the same strike prices but with different expiration dates. Set one spread to expire in one week, another in two weeks, and the last in four weeks. Monitor the performance of each spread and analyze how time decay and volatility affect them differently.

3. **Strategy Planning**: Develop a bull put spread from start to finish. This includes selecting the stock, determining the strike prices, and choosing the expiration dates. Formulate a risk management strategy that outlines how you will adjust the trade if it does not go as planned. Share your plan with a trading mentor or a peer for feedback to enhance it further.

These exercises are designed to promote deeper engagement with the material, helping you think critically and strategically about bull put spreads. As you work through these tasks, keep in mind that each step builds your confidence and competence in navigating the options trading landscape.

CHAPTER 7

BEAR CALL SPREADS

PROFITING FROM A FALLING MARKET

BULL PUT OPTIONS ARE a great choice when the market is on the rise, but what happens when things take a downward turn? That's where the bear call spread comes in! This strategy lets you earn profits if the market stays flat or even dips further. It's perfect for traders who are expecting a drop or just some sideways movement and want a little cushion in case the stock unexpectedly bounces back.

In this chapter, I'll walk you through the basics of a bear call spread, share some examples, and help you feel confident in using this strategy. By the end, you'll have the insights and tools to add bear call spreads to your trading toolkit, making it easier for you to make smart and potentially profitable trades. Let's jump right in!

7.1 Bear Call Structure

A BEAR CALL SPREAD is an options trading strategy that involves selling a call option to collect the premium and then using a portion of that premium to buy another call option with a higher strike price, both having the same expiration date. The higher strike call serves as a hedge, limiting your potential losses. You'll achieve the best profit if the stock price stays below the strike price of the call you sold by the time expiration arrives.

To set up a bear call spread, start by choosing a stock that you believe will remain stable or decline in value. Next, identify resistance levels, these are price points where the stock usually struggles and changes direction. Position your short call strike at or just above these resistance levels.

Then, determine the width of your spread by selecting a strike price for your long call based on the level of risk you are comfortable taking. The difference between your two strike prices will determine your maximum risk. Finally, ensure that both options have the same expiration date.

7.2 Calculating Profits

Let's catch up with Jane, our savvy trader, and her friend Steve. Jane has had some great success trading bull puts on XYZ, but she's feeling a bit anxious after hearing some recent news that suggests the stock might take a downturn. Steve, who's also feeling bearish about XYZ, encourages Jane to consider selling calls.

Right now, XYZ is priced at $122.65. Steve decides to sell a call option with a $125 strike price, earning $2.50 per share (that's $250 for each contract!). He's hopeful that the stock will drop, which would let him keep his profit. As long as XYZ stays below $125, he's in a good spot!

However, he does have to keep in mind that he's now committed to selling 100 shares at $125. If the stock price jumps above that strike price, he'll have to buy shares at the higher price to meet his obligation, which would lead to a loss when he sells them.

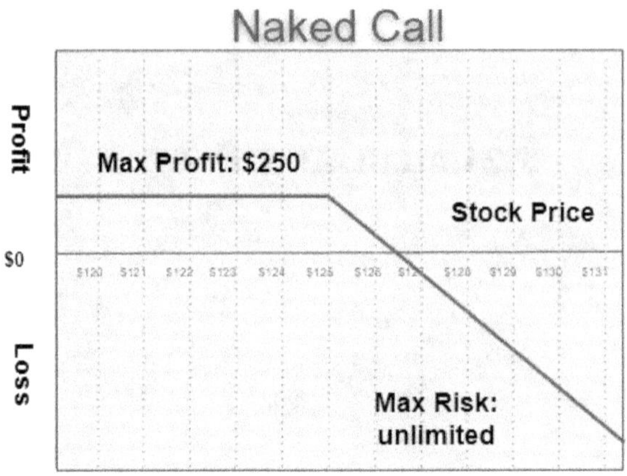

Jane is not comfortable with the idea of placing a trade that involves potentially unlimited risk. Therefore, she decides to create a bear call spread instead.

In this strategy, Jane sells four call options with a $125 strike price for $2.50 per share and simultaneously buys four call options with a $130 strike price for $1.00 per share.

To calculate her maximum profit, she finds the difference between the credit received from the short calls ($2.50) and the debit paid for the long calls ($1.00). This difference is then multiplied by 100 (since each contract represents 100 shares) and further multiplied by the number of contracts (4).

Bear Call Profit

Short Call Credit - Long Call Debit = **Net Credit**

Net Credit * Total Contracts = **Max Profit**

Here's how it breaks down:

- **Short Call Credit:** $2.50
- **Long Call Debit:** $1.00
- **Net Credit:** $1.50 per share

- **Maximum Profit:** $1.50 x 100 shares x 4 contracts = $600

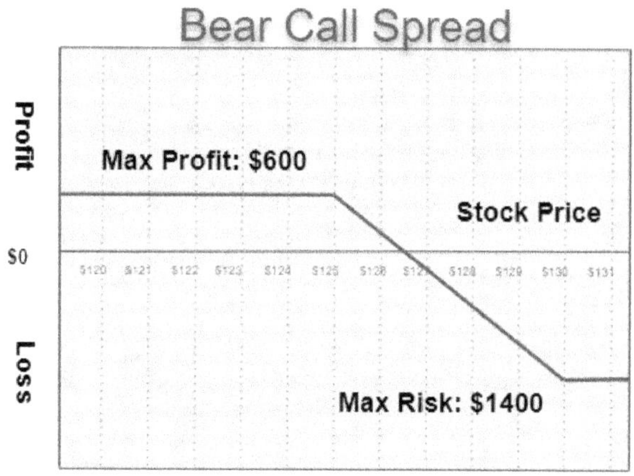

As long as XYZ stays below $125, all options will expire worthless, allowing Jane to secure a profit of $600. If the stock price rises above $125, her profit will decrease, but her risk is limited by the $130 strike long calls she purchased.

7.3 CALCULATING RISKS

AS WE DISCUSSED PREVIOUSLY, not all trades go as planned, so it is essential to understand the risks associated with any trade you enter.

How much is Jane risking to potentially earn a $600 profit? While Steve's naked calls carry unlimited risk, Jane's bear call spreads are much more conservative. Each short call exposes her to the obligation to sell 100 shares at $125, while each long call gives her the right to buy 100 shares at $130. Jane is trading four short calls at the $125 strike price, which means she could be obligated to sell 400 shares at $125 each. However, she is not risking $50,000. Why is that?

Bear Call Risk

Long Call Strike - Short Call Strike = **Spread**

(Spread - Net Credit) * Total Contracts = **Max Risk**

Jane's maximum loss is capped at the difference between the strike price of her short call and her long call ($5), minus the net credit she received when opening the trade ($1.50). This means her maximum loss is $3.50 per share or $350 per contract. With four contracts, her total risk amounts to only $1,400.

In contrast, Steve needs to maintain a margin account to cover the potentially unlimited risk of his naked calls. Jane's broker, however, knows exactly how much capital Jane has at risk and only requires her to set aside $1,400 for this trade.

So, who is in a better position, Jane or Steve? Jane's bear call spread limits her risk to $1,400 while offering a potential profit of $600, resulting in a Return on Risk (ROR) of 42.9%. Although Steve's naked calls could provide a higher profit per contract, they also face unlimited risk if the stock price significantly increases. Consequently, it is impossible to calculate Steve's Return on Risk because his maximum loss is infinite.

7.4 Bear Call Probability Calculations

A bear call is typically designed so that the maximum risk is higher than the maximum reward. This is because a bear call can be a high-probability strategy. It's essential to strike the right balance between potential profit, risk, and probability for long-term success. Remember the Risk, Reward, and Probability triangle from the last chapter.

Let's explore two bear call spreads and see how altering the strike prices impacts risk, reward, and the probability of success.

Equity Trading at $220.27

Trade #1: ITM Bear Call Spread 30 DTE

- **Short Call Strike:** $210, Bid: $13.55, Delta: -.76, Gamma: -.02 , Theta: .11, Vega: -.20
- **Long Call Strike:** $215, Ask: $10.10, Delta: .66, Gamma: .02, Theta: -.12, Vega: .19
- **Max Profit:** $3.45 per share
- **Max Risk:** $1.55 per share

Trade #2: OTM Bear Call Spread 30 DTE

- **Short Call Strike:** $230, Bid: $3.15, Delta: -.31, Gamma: -.02, Theta: .11, Vega: -.23
- **Long Call Strike:** $235, Ask: $2.08, Delta: .22, Gamma: .02, Theta: -.09, Vega: .22
- **Max Profit:** $1.07 per share
- **Max Risk:** $3.93 per share

In both scenarios, the short call is approximately $10 away from the current stock price, and the options expire in 30 days, but they have very different risk profiles.

Trade #1 offers a higher maximum profit of $3.45 per share and a lower maximum risk of just $1.55 per share. However, since it's an in-the-money (ITM) trade, it has a lower probability of success. For this trade to achieve maximum profit, the stock must drop below $210. If the stock price remains the same, increases, or only drops slightly, this trade will result in a loss.

Trade #2, on the other hand, has a lower maximum profit of $1.07 per share and a higher maximum risk of $3.93 per share. However, because this is an out-of-the-money (OTM) trade, it has a higher probability of success. As long as the equity stays below $230, the trade will achieve its maximum profit. This means the stock doesn't need to decline much, or at all, for this trade to be profitable.

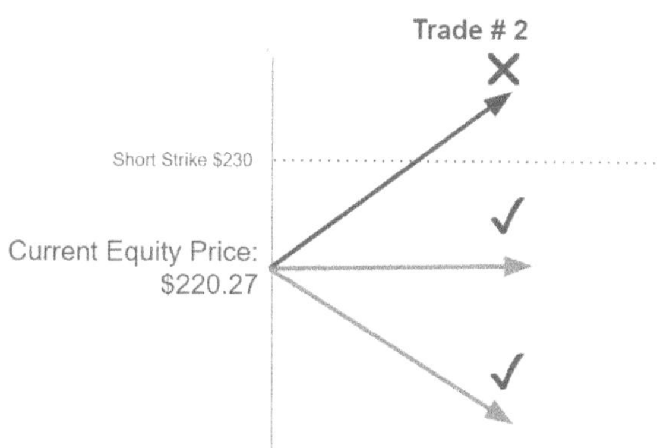

The equity can exceed your short-call strike price, and the trade can still generate a partial profit as long as the equity does not surpass your breakeven point. To calculate the breakeven point for a bear call spread, simply add the net premium received to the strike price of the short call.

For Trade #1, the breakeven point is calculated as follows: $210 (strike price) + $3.45 (net premium received) = $213.45. If the stock remains above $213.45 at expiration, the trade will incur a loss. Conversely, if it finishes below $213.45, the trade will yield some level of profit, achieving maximum profit if the equity is below $210 at expiration.

Trade #2 collects a lower premium, which means it will transition from a profitable trade to a losing position more quickly if the equity breaches the short-call strike price. The breakeven point for Trade #2 is $230 (strike price) + $1.07 (net premium received) = $231.07. This trade will achieve maximum profit as long as the equity stays below $230 and will remain partially profitable as long as the equity is below $231.07.

7.5 Bear Call Greeks

Now, let's explore the Greeks to understand their impact on a bear call spread, how this strategy generates profits, and what challenges it may encounter.

We'll use the Greeks from Trade #2 as an example:

- **Short Call Strike:** $230, Bid: $3.15, Delta: -.31, Gamma: -.02, Theta: .11, Vega: -.23
- **Long Call Strike:** $235, Ask: $2.08, Delta: .22, Gamma: .02, Theta: -.09, Vega: .22

First, let's calculate the Net Greeks by combining the Greek values of the short and long options, then multiplying by the number of contracts. For simplicity, we'll look at just one contract:

- **Net Position Delta:** -.31 (short call) + .22 (long call) = -.09
- **Net Position Gamma:** -.02 (short call) + .02 (long call) = 0
- **Net Position Theta:** .11 (short call) + -.09 (long call) = .02
- **Net Position Vega:** -.23 (short call) + .22 (long call) = -.01

To convert these into per-contract values, multiply each by 100:

- **Net Position Delta:** -9
- **Net Position Gamma:** 0
- **Net Position Theta:** 2
- **Net Position Vega:** -1

Here's what these Greeks indicate:

- **Delta** is negative, which means that this position will lose value if the underlying stock rises and gain value if the stock trends lower.
- **Gamma** is neutral, suggesting that there will be minimal impact on Delta as the stock moves up or down, at least in the short term. This value will change quickly as time ticks forward or the price of the underlying equity changes.
- **Theta** is positive, indicating that this trade benefits from time decay, as options lose value over time, which works in your favor.
- **Vega** is negative, meaning the trade will lose value if implied volatility increases and gain value if implied volatility decreases.

Understanding these Greeks lets you anticipate how your trade will react to various market conditions, helping you manage your position more effectively.

7.6 When to Use Bear Call Spreads

When both your technical indicators, such as moving averages or the MACD (Moving Average Convergence Divergence), and your fundamental analysis suggest that a stock might decline, it often creates a good opportunity for a bear call spread. Ideally, you should be looking for stocks that are trending downward or, at the very least, are unlikely to rise.

Your analytical skills can be crucial in this process. For instance, weak earnings reports or challenges within the industry may indicate that a stock is losing value. On the technical side, tools like moving averages and MACD can signal the beginning of a downtrend.

When both your fundamental and technical analyses align in this manner, it's a strong indication that it's the right time to set up a bear call spread.

7.7 Monitoring and Managing the Trade

Once you've set up your bear call spread, it's important to monitor it, but there's no need to track every minor price change. Setting up a few alerts on your trading platform can keep you informed about significant price shifts or news that may affect the stock. You can also perform technical checks to ensure the stock's performance aligns with your original strategy. If the price begins to approach the strike price of your short call, it's a good time to review your strategy.

Adjusting your spread as the market moves can help you manage potential losses or create opportunities for new gains. If the stock moves against you, but you believe it's a temporary situation, you might consider rolling the trade. This involves closing your current position and opening a new one with different strike prices or a longer expiration in the same transaction. Rolling the trade allows you to reset your setup, providing a fresh perspective that could help you recover or even achieve a profit. On the other hand, if the stock experiences a rapid decline, closing your position early could secure your gains while they are still available. The key is to evaluate whether to hold out for more profit or to take what you have and move on.

7.8 Challenge Your Knowledge

It's time to test your understanding of bear call spreads. Here are some questions to help you assess how well you've grasped the key concepts:

- If the stock price falls significantly a week after you open a bear call spread, what might be a smart action to take with your position?
- How would a sudden increase in implied volatility affect the value of a bear call spread?
- What is the significance of the breakeven point in a bear call spread, and how do you calculate it?
- Why is it important to consider the earnings report dates for the stock when setting up a bear call spread?
- How does the choice of expiration date influence the risk level of your bear call spread?
- What are some signs that it might be time to close your bear call spread before its expiration?

Practical Exercises

Here are some exercises to help you practice what you've learned and gain more confidence with bear call spreads:

1. **Market Simulation:** Choose a stock that you think will either decline or remain stable. Based on current market data, select the most appropriate strike prices and expiration dates for a bear call spread. Track this virtual trade over a week, noting how different market shifts affect the spread.

2. **Exploring Variations:** Select a stock that you believe will decrease in value. Using a virtual trading platform or a spreadsheet, create three bear call spreads for this stock with the same strike prices but different expiration dates. Set one to expire in one week, another in two weeks, and the last in four weeks. Observe how time decay impacts each trade and how changes in implied volatility affect them differently.

3. **Strategy Planning:** Develop a detailed plan for a bear call spread, including your criteria for selecting the stock, determining the strike prices, and choosing the expiration dates. Outline a risk management strategy, noting potential adjustments and the situations that would trigger those changes. Share your plan with a trading buddy or mentor to receive feedback and refine your approach.

These exercises are designed to enhance your understanding and encourage critical thinking about bear call spreads. Engaging in them will help build your confidence and skills in options trading.

CHAPTER 8

IRON CONDORS

STRATEGY FOR MARKET NEUTRALITY

THE BULL PUT SPREAD is a great strategy for a market that's either stagnant or trending upwards, while the bear call spread works well in a stagnant or bearish market. As you've been going through the previous chapters, you might have thought, "Hey, since both of these trades can make money in a flat market, why not use them together to boost my returns?" If that thought crossed your mind, congratulations! You've just stumbled upon the iron condor.

An iron condor allows you to generate higher profits compared to other credit spreads when the market remains relatively flat, meaning it isn't significantly moving up or down. This versatile tool can provide a steady income while keeping your risk controlled.

In this chapter, I will break down the mechanics of the iron condor, walk you through examples, and demonstrate how to effectively use this strategy. Additionally, we'll compare it to a similar but higher-risk strategy called a naked strangle. By the end of this chapter, you will have a solid understanding of how to incorporate iron condors into your trading toolkit, enabling you to make more strategic and profitable decisions in the market. Let's dive in!

8.1 Understanding the Iron Condor

An iron condor is a strategy that combines two techniques you've already learned: the bull put spread and the bear call spread. When you set up an iron condor, you are essentially placing a bull put spread below the current market price and a bear call spread above it at the same time. This creates a four-legged options strategy that profits when the stock stays within a specific price range.

Here's how it works: First, identify an equity that is trading within a range. Then, determine the levels of support and resistance. Sell a bear call spread with the short call strike at or above the resistance level and simultaneously sell a bull put spread with the short put strike at or below the support level.

The maximum profit occurs if the stock price remains between the strike prices of the short call and short put at expiration. The iron condor limits both your upside and downside risk while providing the opportunity for a higher profit as long as the equity remains range-bound or stagnant.

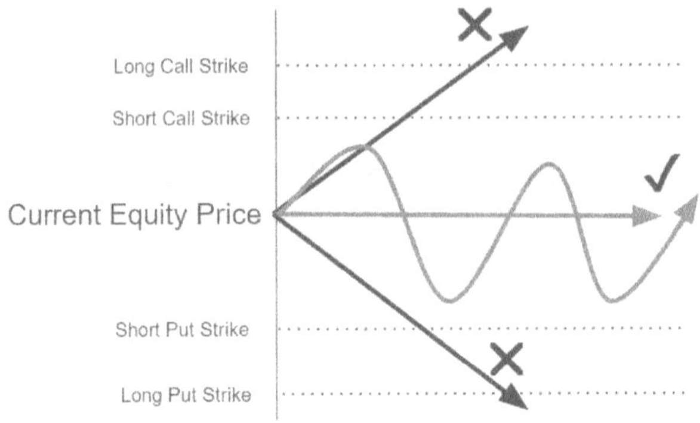

The distance between the strike prices of your short options determines the range of values at which the equity can land at expiration to yield a maximum profit. A wider distance results in a larger range, increasing the likelihood **of closing** the trade successfully for a profit. However, when your short options are further out of the money, the premium you can collect decreases, which subsequently lowers your maximum potential profit.

On the other hand, narrowing the distance between your short options brings them closer to the at-the-money price. This approach reduces the probability of profit but increases the **maximum** potential return.

Your risk is defined by the distance between your short and long options, for whichever side has the greater spread. If both sides are equal, the maximum risk is simply the value of the spread minus the credit received.

8.2 CALCULATING PROFITS AND RISKS

LET'S REVISIT JANE AND Steve. Jane has successfully traded both bull put spreads and bear call spreads, and she is quickly outperforming her friend Steve, who only uses single-option strategies. This time, they have noticed that XYZ has been trading within a range for a while; it's currently priced at $160.34. They have identified support at $150 and resistance at $175, and they expect the stock to remain within this range for the next few weeks.

Steve decides to sell a naked put and a naked call simultaneously, creating a naked strangle. He sells a naked call option with a strike price of $175, 32 days out, for $3.00 per share, and a naked put option at the $150 strike for $3.15 per share. This gives him a maximum profit of $6.15 per share or $615 in total.

On the bearish side, Steve is risking $14,385; however, since his trade includes a naked call, his risk on the bullish side is potentially unlimited.

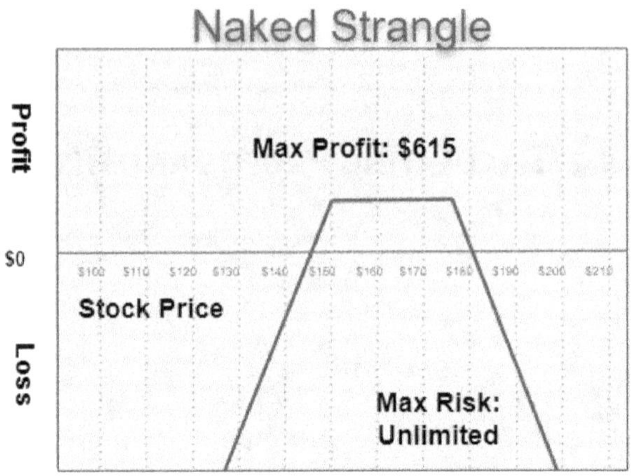

Jane recognizes that both bull put spreads and bear call spreads could be profitable in this scenario. Therefore, she decides to set up both simultaneously, creating an iron condor.

On the call side of her trade, Jane sells four short calls with a strike price of $175, which brings in $3.00 per share. To limit her risk, she purchases four long calls with a strike price of $180 for $2.15 per share.

On the put side, she sells four short puts with a strike price of $150, generating $3.15 per share, and buys four long puts with a strike price of $145 at a cost of $2.03 per share. All options are set to expire in 32 days.

Iron Condor Profit

Bear Call Credit + Bull Put Credit = **Net Credit**

Net Credit * Total Contracts = **Max Profit**

Here's the breakdown:

- **Bear Call Spread Credit:** $3.00 (short call) - $2.15 (long call) = $0.85 per share
- **Bull Put Spread Credit:** $3.15 (short put) - $2.03 (long put) = $1.12

per share

- **Total Iron Condor Credit Received:** \$0.85 + \$1.12 = \$1.97 per share
- **Maximum Profit:** \$1.97 x 100 shares x 4 contracts = \$788

Jane's maximum profit of \$788 is realized if XYZ is between \$150 and \$175 at expiration.

8.3 PROBABILITY AND BREAKEVEN CALCULATIONS

IRON CONDORS RELY ON the stock price staying within a specific range, so a significant move up or down can disrupt the trade. This strategy has two breakeven points: one above and one below the current price. Understanding how to calculate these breakeven points helps you maintain control over the trade.

To determine the breakeven points for an iron condor, consider both sides of the trade:

- **Upper Breakeven:** Start with the strike price of the short call and add the net credit received. For example, Jane sold a $175 short call and collected a total of $1.97 per share from the iron condor. Therefore:
  - $175 + $1.97 = **$176.97**
- **Lower Breakeven:** Take the strike price of the short put and subtract the net credit received. Jane sold a $150 short put and also collected $1.97 per share from the iron condor. Thus:
  - $150 - $1.97 = **$148.03**

Jane's Iron Condor will be profitable at expiration if the equity is priced anywhere between $148.03 and $176.97. If the stock moves outside this range, Jane will start to incur losses, but her long options cap her potential losses.

Now, let's examine the probabilities:

- **Probability of Expiring In The Money (ITM):** The delta of the short call and short put can provide a rough estimate of the probability that the options will expire in the money, which could lead to a loss. A higher delta indicates a higher potential profit, whereas a lower delta suggests a greater likelihood of success. In this example, the $175 short call had a delta of 0.27, and the short put had a delta of 0.25, giving this trade a 73% probability of reaching its maximum profit based on delta alone.

In this example, the bull call option is targeting a 20% return on risk (ROR) based on a $0.85 premium against a $4.15 potential loss. The bull put option is aiming for a 28.9% ROR with a $1.12 premium against a $3.88 potential loss. But what is Jane's overall ROR on the Iron Condor strategy?

It's important to note that you cannot simply add the individual returns together to arrive at a total ROR of 48.9%. In the case of an Iron Condor, the whole is greater than the sum of its parts.

To determine the return on risk effectively, we first need to calculate the total risk of the entire position. An Iron Condor can incur losses if the underlying equity moves outside the predefined range in either direction. However, it is important to understand that it is impossible to lose on both sides simultaneously— the equity cannot end up above the upper breakeven point and below the lower breakeven point at the same time. Therefore, one side of the trade will always be profitable.

The worst-case scenario for Jane is that she loses on one side while winning on the other. Consequently, to calculate her maximum potential loss for the whole position, she only needs to consider the risk from one side of the trade.

- **Maximum Risk:** The width of each spread is $5.00, so the maximum risk is $5.00 - $1.97 (net credit) = $3.03 per share.
- **Total Risk:** $3.03 x 100 shares per contract x 4 contracts = $1,212

Iron Condor Risk

Bear Call Spread or Bull Put Spread (whichever is greater) - Net Credit = **Max Risk**

Jane is risking $1,212 to potentially make $788, giving her a Return on Risk (ROR) of 65%!

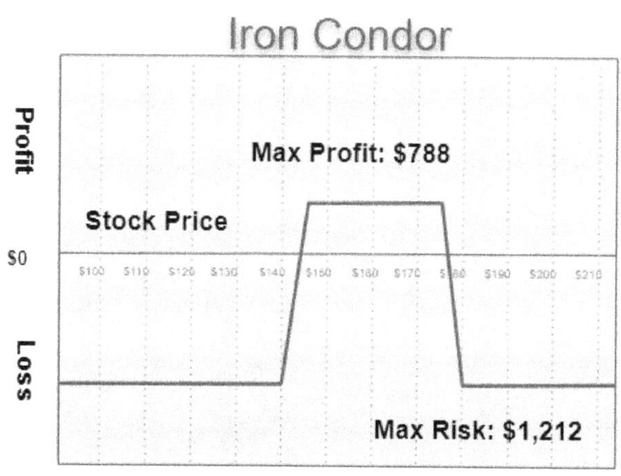

Pro Tip: When determining the risk capital required for an iron condor, it's straightforward: if both sides have the same distance between the short and long strikes, you can select either side. However, if one side has a wider spread, you must use that side to calculate your risk.

8.4 Managing Greeks in an Iron Condor

The Greeks are essential for understanding how your iron condor will react to changes in the market. Let's break down the Greeks for Jane's iron condor:

- **Delta:** Initially, the net delta will be close to zero, which is ideal when you expect the stock to remain range-bound. However, if the equity trends in either direction, you may need to adjust your options to restore a delta-neutral position.
- **Gamma:** The gamma is also close to zero initially because the delta doesn't change much with small price movements. However, gamma will increase as the underlying equity price approaches one of the short strikes, making the position more sensitive to further price changes.
- **Theta:** Iron condors are theta-positive, meaning they benefit from time decay. As the options approach expiration, the extrinsic value decreases, which works to your advantage.
- **Vega:** Iron condors are vega-negative, meaning they lose value if implied volatility increases. A rise in volatility raises the value of the options, which is detrimental to your position since the short options are your primary instruments.

8.5 When to Use an Iron Condor

The ideal time to implement an iron condor strategy is when you expect a stock or the broader market to remain within a specific price range. This scenario often occurs during periods of low volatility, such as after a significant event when the market has settled down, or when there are no major announcements or economic changes anticipated in the near future. The strategy benefits from these conditions because it capitalizes on the lack of movement, allowing you to profit as time decay reduces the option premiums you've sold.

For example, consider a company that has just released its quarterly earnings report, a pivotal event that typically leads to significant price fluctuations before the announcement. However, afterward, the stock price may stabilize as uncertainty fades and traders adjust to the new information. In this post-event lull, using an iron condor can be an effective way to take advantage of the stock's stabilization. By setting up the strategy with short strikes that bracket the expected trading range, you can generate income as the stock price remains within your predicted boundaries.

The beauty of the iron condor lies in its ability to generate profits without requiring the stock to make dramatic moves in either direction. Instead, your goal is for the stock price to stay comfortably within the range defined by the short call and put strikes, allowing you to capture the maximum premium as time passes. This makes the strategy particularly appealing in markets where significant shifts are unlikely, enabling you to leverage your market outlook while effectively managing risk.

8.6 Watching and Adjusting Your Iron Condor

Once your iron condor is set up, the next step is to monitor it, but you don't need to watch it constantly. Instead, consider setting up alerts to notify you if the stock price approaches your breakeven points or if there's a sudden increase in volatility.

Adjusting your iron condor involves managing the Greeks as the stock price changes. If the price gets close to one of your short strikes, you may want to roll the position up or down to align with the current market conditions. Alternatively, if you're confident that the stock will remain stable, you could close out just one side of the position.

You might also decide to close the entire position early if the stock has stayed within your desired range and you've achieved most of your expected profit. Locking in those gains before expiration can help reduce the risk of unexpected market shifts and free up capital for your next trade.

8.7 Test Your Knowledge

Do you think you have a solid understanding of iron condors? Let's test your knowledge with a few questions:

- If volatility suddenly spikes, how might that impact the strike prices you choose for an iron condor?
- How would selecting different expiration dates affect the risk and potential return of your iron condor?
- Why might a trader consider closing an iron condor early, and what factors would influence that decision?
- What happens to the trade profile if the spread between the call and put strike prices widens?
- In which market conditions might an iron condor be less effective, and what alternative strategies could be a better fit?
- When might it make sense to adjust or close one side of the iron condor early?

Practical Exercises

To solidify your understanding of iron condors, try these exercises:

1. **Virtual Trading Setup**: Use a trading simulator to create an iron condor on a stock of your choice. Track this virtual trade for at least a month, paying attention to how price changes and volatility shifts affect the position. Adjust the trade as needed using the strategies covered here, and document your decisions and the outcomes.

2. **Market Analysis Exercise**: Select a stock and review its price movements over the last six months. Identify any low-volatility periods where an iron condor might have performed well. Based on this analysis, plan a hypothetical iron condor setup, noting your chosen strike prices and expiration dates. Explain why you selected these parameters and how you expect the stock to behave.

3. **Risk Management Review**: Reflect on the specific risk management tactics for iron condors. Create a checklist of actions you would take to monitor and adjust the position if the price or volatility changes significantly. Consider how these steps fit into your overall trading plan.

These exercises are designed to encourage critical thinking about iron condors and promote a hands-on approach to mastering this strategy.

In Closing: As we conclude this chapter on iron condors, remember that success with credit spreads is all about balancing risk and reward while remaining attuned to market conditions. The insights you've gained extend beyond individual strategies; they involve understanding market dynamics and solid risk management, which are valuable skills applicable to many trading scenarios.

CHAPTER 9

RISK MANAGEMENT AND TRADE ADJUSTMENTS

IN OPTIONS TRADING, a well-thought-out risk management plan is not just helpful; it's essential for long-term success. The markets can be unpredictable, and without a strategy to mitigate losses, even the most promising trades can quickly turn against you. A solid risk management plan acts as a safety net, ensuring that no single trade can jeopardize your overall portfolio. By clearly defining your risk tolerance and setting boundaries, you position yourself to weather market fluctuations without derailing your trading goals.

Stop-loss orders are one of the most effective tools in this plan, serving as a safeguard to automatically limit potential losses. They provide a structured way to exit a trade when the market moves against you, preventing emotions like fear or greed from clouding your judgment. Instead of holding onto a losing position in the hope that it will recover, a stop-loss order takes the guesswork out of the equation, helping you stick to your plan and protect your capital.

Beyond protection, stop-loss orders contribute to overall trade stability by keeping losses manageable and predictable. This disciplined approach allows you to focus on identifying new opportunities without being weighed down by the emotional and financial impact of significant losses. When incorporated into a broader risk management strategy, stop-loss orders become a powerful ally, enabling you to trade with greater confidence and control, even in the face of market uncertainty.

9.1 Setting Stop-Loss Points

Stop-Loss Orders Explained

A stop-loss order is an instruction to your broker to buy or sell an asset once it reaches a specific price. This order is designed to help you stick to your trading plan and avoid making hasty decisions due to sudden market shifts.

How to Set Stop-Loss Points

Setting an effective stop-loss requires understanding the market and recognizing your own risk tolerance. Here's a guide to help you get started:

1. **Know Your Risk Tolerance**: Before placing any trade, determine what percentage of your total capital you are comfortable risking. Many experienced traders limit this to 1-2% per trade. Although it may be tempting to take on higher risks with newer or smaller portfolios,

doing so can lead to quick and costly losses if trades do not go as planned.

2. **Check Volatility**: Analyze historical and implied volatility to understand how a stock typically moves. This information can help you set a stop-loss that accommodates normal price fluctuations, preventing it from triggering too soon during minor swings.

3. **Match the Time Frame**: If you are trading on a short-term basis, consider tighter stop-loss levels. In contrast, longer-term trades can allow for more room. Day traders often set closer stop-losses, while swing traders may leave a bit more space for movement.

Types of Stop-Loss Orders

Understanding the different types of stop-loss orders can help you refine your trading strategy:

- **Standard Stop-Loss**: This order triggers a sale when the asset's price reaches a specific point. It's straightforward and typically doesn't incur extra fees. However, it does not guarantee an exact fill price; it simply initiates the sale to close the trade.

- **Trailing Stop**: A trailing stop functions like a standard stop-loss but adjusts as the asset's price changes, based on a set percentage or dollar value. This method can be effective for securing profits as the asset rises or falls while also providing protection against sudden moves in the opposite direction. Keep in mind that it does not guarantee a specific fill price.

- Guaranteed Stop: This type of stop-loss offers added peace of mind by ensuring the trade closes at your chosen price, even in volatile market conditions. The drawback is that a "stop premium" may be applied if the stop is activated.

Examples of Stop-Loss Strategies

For Stock Trades:

- **Day Trading**: Suppose you buy shares of a company when the stock is trading at $100. You can set a stop-loss at $95, allowing you to profit if the stock grows while limiting your exposure to the downside.
- **Swing Trading**: If you plan to hold a position for a longer period, consider using a trailing stop, such as setting it around 10% below the purchase price. For example, if the stock rises from $100 to $120, the stop-loss will adjust from $90 to $108, helping you retain gains while still protecting your investment against unexpected downturns.

For Credit Spreads:

- **Fixed Stop-Loss on a Bull Put**: Imagine you sell a bull put spread on a stock currently trading at $150. You sell the $145 put and buy the $140 put for protection, collecting a premium of $1.50. You can set a stop-loss to exit the trade if the spread value reaches $3.00. This approach helps manage your risk by automatically closing the trade if the stock price starts to move against you before you reach the maximum loss.
- Trailing Stop on a Bear Call: Suppose you have a bear call spread on a stock trading at $200, for which you collected a $2 premium. If the spread value drops to $1.00, setting a trailing stop at $1.50 allows you to secure profits while still providing room for adjustments in case the trend changes.

In options trading, managing risk is as crucial as pursuing profits. Incorporating stop-loss strategies helps protect your capital and promotes a steady, disciplined approach.

9.2 Adjusting Spreads When Markets Move

STOP-LOSS ORDERS ARE HELPFUL, but they shouldn't be your only method for managing a trade that doesn't go as planned. Consider adjustments as a way to subtly modify your strategy to align it better with changing market conditions. Learning to adjust your trades will enable you to maintain control and respond proactively as circumstances evolve.

Knowing When to Adjust

Significant changes in stock prices or increased volatility often indicate that an adjustment may be necessary. For instance, if a stock suddenly drops after an earnings report, you might need to modify your trade. However, not every minor fluctuation requires a response. Over-adjusting your trades can be just as harmful as failing to make adjustments. Keep in mind that time decay benefits credit spreads, so a short-term move might not necessitate any changes. Sometimes, the best strategy is to hold your position and wait it out unless something substantial occurs.

Different Ways to Adjust

Adjusting your trade will depend on your initial expectations and any changes that have occurred. One common method of adjustment is called "rolling." This involves closing the current spread and opening a new one within the same transaction. You can choose to roll up or roll down, depending on market conditions. The credit from your new spread should help offset any losses from the original trade. Sometimes, this may require "rolling out," meaning you extend the expiration date to give the trade more time to work and increase the amount of premium you collect. Rolling can be especially beneficial if you believe the movement that threatened the initial trade is temporary.

For example, if you have a bull put spread and the stock starts to drop close to the strike price of the short put, you might choose to roll the bull put to a lower strike price and extend the expiration date. On the other hand, if you're in a bear call spread and the stock price rises, rolling the spread up and out could be advantageous.

In some situations, it may be best to take ownership of the stock. This allows you to convert the position into a long-term investment or change it into something like a covered call.

Examples

If a trader sets up a bear call strategy on a tech stock, anticipating that the stock price will remain stable, and then the company announces a new product that drives the stock price higher, the trader might expect this bullish trend to continue. To adapt to this situation, the trader could preemptively buy shares, effectively converting the bear call into a covered call. This strategy helps protect against potential losses from continued bullish movement, while the long call position could generate additional profits if the stock continues to rise.

Conversely, if a trader has a bull put spread and the market suddenly drops, but they believe the market will rebound or stabilize in the near future, they can consider rolling the spread down and extending the expiration date. This adjustment can help keep the position manageable by allowing more time for the stock to recover, thus preserving the overall trade.

The following flowcharts can serve as a guide to help you plan adjustments when the market moves unexpectedly.

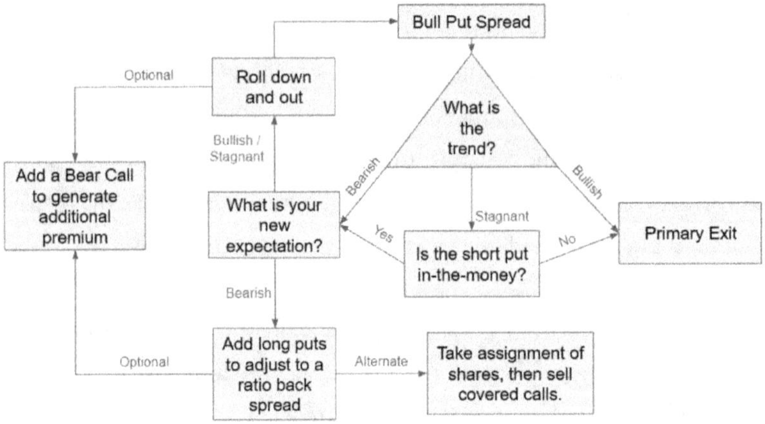
Bull Put Spread
What is the trend?
Bearish
Bullish
Stagnant
Is the short put in-the-money?
Yes
No
Primary Exit
What is your new expectation?
Bullish / Stagnant
Roll down and out
Optional
Add a Bear Call to generate additional premium
Bearish
Add long puts to adjust to a ratio back spread
Optional
Alternate
Take assignment of shares, then sell covered calls.

Bear Call Spread
What is the trend?
Bullish
Bearish
Stagnant
Is the short call in-the-money?
Yes
No
Primary Exit
What is your new expectation?
Bearish / Stagnant
Roll up and out
Optional
Add a Bull Put to generate additional premium
Bullish
Buy long calls to adjust to a ratio back spread.
Optional
Alternate
Buy shares to adjust to a covered call with a long call for additional upside potential.

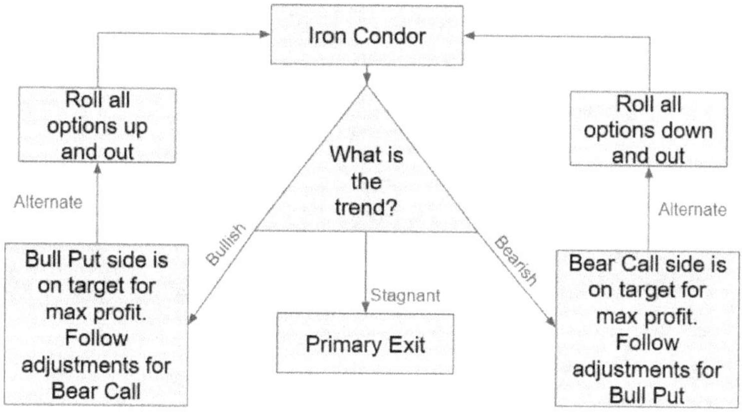

Effective adjustments keep your trade in line with your expectations, allowing you to respond to market fluctuations as they occur.

9.3 Recognizing When to Make Trade Adjustments

Positions can be adjusted to reduce or limit losses or to increase and lock in gains. Adjusting is all about staying in sync with the market and understanding when a small change can lead to a significant difference.

Major market news events often serve as obvious triggers. For instance, if the CEO of a company you're trading is involved in a scandal, the stock may decline. In such cases, you would need to make adjustments to minimize potential losses on any bullish positions or shift to bearish trades to profit from the new trend. Unexpected market movements, where stock shifts sharply in an unanticipated direction, require reevaluating your positions. Consider situations where a stock unexpectedly breaks through a resistance level or falls below a support level; failing to adjust your expectations and strategy according to the new information can lead to more losing trades.

A rapid move in a favorable direction may prompt you to reposition your trade to lock in profits, ensuring you don't lose gains if the market suddenly reverses. Additionally, upcoming earnings announcements can create volatility that might necessitate strategic adjustments in your positions, either to prepare for uncertainty or to capitalize on potential quick gains.

If you notice an unusual increase in trading volume that pushes the stock past a certain level, it's wise to take a step back, reassess, and determine if your initial expectations are still valid or if adjustments are necessary to align the trade with your new outlook.

How Adjustments Shift Your Trade's Balance

Adjusting a trade can affect both the risk and reward aspects of your strategy. For example, if you roll a long put down a few points after the stock has turned bearish, you can lock in some profits. This adjustment offers added safety in case of a reversal, but it also comes with a trade-off. Specifically, it reduces your maximum potential profit. Since each adjustment has its own advantages and disadvantages, it's important to consider what each change adds or takes away to ensure it aligns with your overall strategy.

More Examples of Trade Adjustments

To understand how trade adjustments can be beneficial and help secure profits, here are a couple of scenarios demonstrating the decision-making process in action.

Imagine a trader who has placed a bull put spread on a tech stock that has a major product launch approaching. Anticipation in the market drives the stock price higher than expected well before the event. Recognizing this early gain, the trader decides to adjust the spread to a higher strike price, allowing him to realize some profit while still positioning for further upside if the stock continues to climb.

In another scenario, a trader has set up an iron condor on an energy stock that suddenly starts to decline after unexpected regulatory news impacts the sector. The trader decides to adjust the bull put side down to a lower strike price and rolls it out to a later expiration date while allowing the bear call to expire. This adjustment enables them to lock in the gains from the bear call and potentially increase profits if the stock stabilizes or rebounds.

While it can be tempting to react to every price change, the goal is to make thoughtful decisions that align with your larger objectives. Flexibility allows you to adapt to market shifts, but maintaining a clear focus on your plan ensures that you stay on track.

9.4 Diversifying Your Portfolio for Smarter Risk Control

Diversification in a trading portfolio involves balancing various assets to manage risk and establish a stronger foundation for potential returns. This concept aligns with the saying, "Don't put all your eggs in one basket." By spreading out investments, if one area underperforms, it will have a limited impact on the entire portfolio.

How Diversification Works

Instead of concentrating on a single stock or industry, it's beneficial to diversify your investments across various sectors. Consider exploring different industries, geographic regions, and asset types so that your entire portfolio isn't negatively impacted if one sector experiences a downturn. For instance, if technology stocks are struggling during a particular week, consumer goods stocks may remain stable. This diversification can significantly reduce the impact of losses from one sector on your overall investments, especially in volatile markets.

Applying Diversification in Options

In options trading, diversification involves using multiple strategies and trading various equities. Avoid being a one-trick pony. Incorporate a mix of spread strategies and different expiration dates. Utilize shorter-term trades for faster returns, while also implementing longer-term strategies for increased stability. Ensure that each trade is a sensible size; this approach minimizes the impact of any single bad trade on your overall portfolio. This balanced strategy can help you manage various types of risk while creating more opportunities.

The Role of Correlation in Diversification

It's important to understand how different assets are linked or "correlated." Correlation indicates how two assets move in relation to each other. For instance, if one stock rises, does another often decline? When assets are closely correlated, they may experience similar changes, which can limit the benefits of diversification. To achieve a better balance in your portfolio, consider including assets with low or negative correlations, such as gold, in a stock-heavy investment strategy. Utilizing tools like a correlation matrix can help visualize these relationships, making it easier to select assets that complement each other effectively.

Routine Check-Ins on Your Portfolio

After you've created a diverse portfolio, it's important to check in on it regularly. Every few months, review your positions to ensure they align with your goals. Markets can change, and it may be beneficial to adjust your holdings or add new investments to maintain balance. During these reviews, evaluate whether your current assets still fit your trading objectives and consider if there are new opportunities that could enhance your portfolio.

9.5 Handling Early Assignment Risk in Options Trading

Imagine you're all set for a relaxing weekend, but then you're unexpectedly called back. That's what early assignment can feel like in trading. If it catches you off guard, it can disrupt your trading plans. Early assignment occurs when an option buyer exercises their option before expiration, forcing the option seller to fulfill their obligation. Understanding why and when this happens is essential for managing your strategy effectively.

Options that are held until expiration will be automatically assigned if they expire in the money, or they will expire worthless if they are out of the money. Early assignment is rare and typically only occurs when it is financially beneficial for the buyer to exercise their option early. A common scenario is when short calls are assigned just before an ex-dividend date. For example, if you hold a short call that is in the money and an ex-dividend date is approaching, the long call holder might choose to exercise their right to buy the shares in order to collect the dividend, especially if the dividend payout exceeds the remaining extrinsic value of the option.

Several factors can increase the likelihood of early assignment. As mentioned, dividends play a significant role, particularly with short calls. Therefore, it's important to keep an eye on the ex-dividend dates for the stocks on which you are selling calls. Similarly, options that are deep in the money, with high intrinsic value and minimal extrinsic value, are more likely to be exercised early, especially as expiration approaches. Selling very short-term options with little extrinsic value also increases the probability of early assignment.

Planning ahead can help mitigate the risk of early assignment. One effective strategy is to select expiration dates that are further out in time and to close positions early rather than holding them until expiration. Although ultra-short-term options may decay faster, they are also more susceptible to early assignment. If you're concerned about this possibility, opt for options with greater time value to help reduce the risk.

If early assignment does occur, having a plan is crucial. First, assess the impact on your portfolio and any obligations resulting from the assignment. For example, if you are assigned on a short call that is part of a bear call spread, your long call can limit your potential loss by allowing you to buy shares at the long call strike price instead of the potentially higher market price, whereas if you are assigned on a naked call, you must purchase shares at the higher market price and immediately sell them at a loss. If you are assigned on a short put that is part of a bull put spread, you'll need to decide whether to hold onto the shares and keep the long put in place as a hedge or sell the shares and close out the put to free up more capital.

Staying calm and following a plan based on your risk assessment and market outlook will help you manage unexpected surprises effectively.

9.6 Understanding the Mindset Behind Options Trading

Regardless of your level of experience, emotions such as fear, greed, and pride can influence your trading decisions. You may feel tempted to exit a trade early because you're afraid of losing the small gains you've already made, or you might hold onto a losing trade too long in the hope that it will turn around. It's normal to let past experiences affect your choices; for instance, after sustaining a significant loss, you may become more cautious, while after a series of wins, you might become overly confident and take unnecessary risks.

Developing emotional resilience can significantly impact your trading performance. Markets fluctuate, and it's essential to remain calm, even when things don't go as expected.

Decision-making under pressure is also a crucial aspect of trading psychology. In moments of high stress, it's easy to react impulsively. That's why having a clear plan is beneficial. Outline your goals, set your risk limits, and establish a basic strategy so you have a solid reference when the market becomes volatile. By setting clear targets for both profits and losses, you can avoid becoming greedy during successful trades or panicking during downturns.

Learning from mistakes is another essential element of trading psychology. Everyone makes errors, but what matters is how you respond to them. Instead of dwelling on a bad trading day, focus on what you can learn from the experience. Was your stop-loss too tight? Did you deviate from your plan? Take notes on what happened and how you felt during the trade. Over time, tracking both your actions and emotions can provide valuable insights and help you identify patterns in your trading behavior.

The psychology behind trading is as vital as data analysis. With the right approach, focusing on emotional resilience, adhering to a plan, and learning from each trade, trading can become not only more effective but also more enjoyable. The ultimate goal is to trade in a way that promotes both financial success and personal peace of mind.

9.7 Creating a Personalized Risk Management Plan

When purchasing a custom suit, every detail, from the fabric to the cut, is tailored to fit you perfectly. Similarly, your risk management plan should be designed to align with your specific trading style, goals, and comfort level with risk. This plan serves as an essential component for maintaining consistency and effectiveness in your trading.

Let's explore the key elements of a solid risk management plan and how you can incorporate them into your trading routine.

Key Parts of Risk Management

A risk management plan primarily addresses three key areas: your comfort level with risk, methods for assessing risk, and strategies for handling it.

Firstly, your risk tolerance indicates the amount of risk you are comfortable taking on, which is influenced by your financial situation, your goals, and your willingness to endure market fluctuations.

Secondly, risk assessment involves understanding the risks associated with your overall trading strategy as well as with individual trades. This includes evaluating past performance, considering the current market climate, and utilizing tools to measure volatility.

Lastly, risk mitigation focuses on actions you can take to minimize risk. This can include planning secondary exit strategies, setting stop-loss orders, diversifying your portfolio, and limiting the size of your positions.

Your trading goals significantly influence how you manage risk. Consider whether you are aiming for long-term growth or seeking quick profits. For instance, a day trader may be more comfortable with volatility, while a retirement account typically prioritizes steady growth. Your goals will shape your approach to assessing and managing risk.

Making It Your Own

To customize this plan for yourself, begin with a "risk audit" of your current setup. Assess the assets you trade and the sizes of your positions. Do these align with your current comfort level regarding risk? If certain trades cause you discomfort, consider making adjustments to better align them with your risk tolerance. This can help manage anxiety and enhance your trading results.

Additionally, take into account where you are in life and what your current needs are. For example, someone nearing retirement should approach risk differently than a younger trader, who has more time to recover from market downturns. Your plan should be flexible enough to adapt as your life circumstances and financial goals change.

Putting the Plan to Work

Incorporating your trading plan into your routine doesn't have to be complicated. Most trading platforms offer automation tools, such as automatic stop-losses and Good 'Til Canceled (GTC) orders, allowing you to avoid constantly monitoring the market. Additionally, portfolio management software can help you track diversification and notify you if a specific area of your portfolio becomes too risky.

Start each day with a quick review of your risk limits and any news that could affect your trades. This practice helps keep you focused and prevents impulsive decisions that may increase your risk exposure.

Ongoing Review and Updates

Just as a suit may require adjustments over time as your midsection expands, your risk management plan will also need updating as your portfolio grows. It's important to review your plan quarterly or every six months. During these reviews, consider any changes in your personal financial situation and ask yourself whether your current strategies still align with your long-term goals.

Additionally, analyze if recent market changes could impact your portfolio. For example, shifts in interest rates, changes in policies, or increased market volatility may signal a need to adjust your strategies. It's also possible that your own goals have shifted, and your trading methodology may need realignment to keep you on track. You might be nearing a specific financial target, allowing you to take on less risk, or you may have become more comfortable with market fluctuations, enabling you to take on a bit more risk.

Updating your risk management plan ensures that it remains effective, helping you keep your losses manageable and stay focused on your personal financial goals. Remember, risk management isn't about avoiding risk entirely; it's about understanding it, managing it, and using it as a tool for growth.

9.8 Test Your Knowledge

Now that you've covered these core concepts let's see how they apply in real scenarios. I've put together a set of questions to help you think like a trader, applying these tools in your day-to-day activities and reinforcing this knowledge as part of your trading toolkit.

- What would you do if you noticed that one of the assets in your diversified portfolio consistently underperforms each quarter?
- How could you implement a risk assessment strategy to determine whether you should invest further in a top-performing asset?
- If you discovered that two of your main investments were more closely linked than you realized, what steps would you take?
- During a period of high market volatility, what factors would you consider when deciding whether to adjust your stop-loss levels?
- If the market started to shift against your position, how would you decide whether to stick to your original plan or make adjustments?
- While reviewing your recent trades, you recognize a pattern of emotional reactions when a trade is challenged. What steps could you take to manage your response more effectively next time?

Practical Exercises

Now, let's put theory into practice. Try these exercises to build both confidence and skills in managing risk and adjusting trades as the market evolves:

1. **Simulation Exercise**: If you have access to a virtual trading platform, set up and adjust at least three different trades. For this exercise, consider the following: initiate a bullish trade on a bearish stock, a bearish trade on a stock showing signs of growth, and a strategy for a stock that is stuck in a range. Use risk management tools like stop-loss orders, alerts, or calculators to make adjustments as needed. This practice will help you understand how different adjustments impact trades, so when the market turns against you in real life, you will be less likely to react emotionally and more equipped to manage it calmly.

2. **Journaling Exercise**: Start or continue a trading journal. For the next month, record each trade you make, noting your reasoning, the risk management techniques you used, and the results. Pay special attention to any adjustments you made during trades—did they work out? Would you take a different approach next time? Reviewing your journal will help you spot patterns and improve your approach to managing risk.

3. **Mentor Feedback**: Arrange a session with a more experienced trader to review your trading and risk management methods. Come prepared with specific questions and areas where you need guidance, and take notes to make the most of their insights. This can be a great way to gain fresh perspectives on managing risk and adjusting trades across

different market conditions.

By actively engaging in these exercises, you will build the skills needed to manage risk confidently and adjust strategies as necessary. Remember, the goal is to develop a trading practice that is steady, adaptable, and aligned with your financial goals.

CHAPTER 10

SUSTAINING LONG-TERM TRADING SUCCESS

IMAGINE CONSTRUCTING A STURDY, reliable sailboat. You've meticulously chosen the finest materials, spent countless hours crafting it, and ensured every detail is prepared for a successful voyage. Yet, as any seasoned sailor knows, the true test comes not from building the boat but from navigating the unpredictable waters ahead. The waves, winds, and storms you encounter will demand adaptability and quick thinking. Trading is no different. While building a strong foundation by mastering strategies and tools is vital, your success ultimately hinges on your ability to adapt and refine your approach in response to ever-changing market conditions.

Just as sailors learn to read the wind and adjust their sails to stay on course, traders must develop a mindset of continuous learning and improvement. The market is dynamic, influenced by countless factors, from economic shifts to technological advancements and even global events. A strategy that works perfectly today might need adjustments tomorrow. Staying sharp requires more than just understanding the basics—it involves actively seeking knowledge, learning from past trades, and staying curious about new developments in the trading world.

Creating a learning plan ensures your skills remain relevant and effective over time. This involves setting aside regular time to review trades, analyze market trends, and explore advanced strategies as you gain experience. It might include reading books, attending webinars, or learning from seasoned traders to deepen your understanding. With a commitment to ongoing growth, you're not just reacting to the market, you're anticipating it, positioning yourself for success even when the waters get rough.

10.1 Building Your Ongoing Learning Plan for Trading

Markets are always on the move, and that means your trading strategies should be too! To keep up with all the changes, it's really important to stay informed. Make it a habit to read a bit every day—whether it's market analysis, trading books, or the latest financial news. This way, you'll be able to spot trends and know what's moving the market

If you're looking to dive deeper, consider signing up for specialized courses. They can really help you sharpen your skills and fill in any knowledge gaps you might not even be aware of. Plus, they're a great way to explore the trading areas that interest you most.

Don't forget about attending online webinars or in-person seminars! These events are fantastic for getting tips directly from seasoned traders and industry experts. You'll pick up new techniques, learn about risk management, and get practical advice that you won't find in textbooks. And who knows? You might even meet some fellow traders in your area to exchange ideas with!

With so much information online, it's important to stick to reliable sources and trading communities where experienced traders share their valuable insights. This will help you filter out the noise and focus on what truly matters.

Setting goals can keep you motivated and on track. Take a look at your current skills and identify where you want to improve. Maybe you want to boost your technical analysis skills or try out a new strategy. Whatever it is, break it down into specific milestones with deadlines, like mastering a tool in three months or learning two new techniques in six months. And remember to adjust your goals as you progress so they stay relevant.

Just remember, staying flexible and committed to learning is what truly helps traders succeed. With a solid plan, reliable resources, and clear goals, you'll be ready to tackle any changes in the market. So keep that curiosity alive, keep learning, and enjoy your trading journey!

10.2 Making the Shift from a Full-Time Job to Part-Time Trading

Transitioning from a steady job to part-time trading involves more than just adjusting your schedule; there is a significant psychological aspect to consider. You must find a way to balance the security of a regular paycheck with the new opportunities that trading presents. Keep in mind that building a stable income from trading takes time. With careful planning, patience, and effective time management, this transition can be manageable.

It's best to start with realistic goals that feel achievable. Work backward from your ideal monthly target, breaking it down into weekly or even daily objectives. Consider the capital you have available, the returns you aim to achieve, and the amount of risk you are comfortable taking. For instance, if your goal is to earn $5,000 a month, estimate how many trades you'd need to execute and the average profit per trade required to reach that target, even if some of the trades don't go as planned. In the beginning, consider reinvesting some of your profits instead of withdrawing everything. This strategy can help grow your account more quickly.

Balancing trading with a full-time job can add extra stress to your life, so it's wise to have methods to unwind and de-stress. Trading often demands quick decisions and carries inherent risks, which can be overwhelming when paired with a regular job. Engaging in a hobby, exercising, or finding other relaxation techniques can help you reset and stay grounded, keeping your mind clear when trading.

The shift to part-time trading is not solely about learning new strategies; it also involves integrating trading into your daily life. With realistic goals, a flexible schedule, and effective stress-management techniques, you can smoothly transition into this new venture without drastically altering your lifestyle.

10.3 Networking with Other Traders: Tips and Benefits

Trading doesn't have to be a lonely journey. Building a network of fellow traders can significantly enhance your experience. When you connect with others who share your interest in trading, it creates a sense of teamwork where everyone can share tips, experiences, and even enjoy some laughs together.

Having a network provides you with a strong support system. Trading is full of ups and downs, often feeling like a rollercoaster ride. Connecting with other traders who understand these challenges can be incredibly helpful. When you're uncertain about a strategy or facing a tough market, a quick chat with a fellow trader can inspire new ideas or offer the encouragement you need to persevere. Listening to others' stories—whether they're successes or mistakes—can also help you avoid some of the trial-and-error learning.

Additionally, networking can introduce you to new strategies and tools that you might not discover on your own. Every trader has a unique style, and learning about the methods others use can open up new possibilities you may not have considered. Sharing ideas in this way can really broaden your perspective on the markets.

Finding Trading Communities

Finding a trading community may seem challenging, but there are many options available. Online forums and social media platforms are filled with trading groups. For instance, Reddit hosts subreddits such as r/StockMarket and r/options, where traders can discuss strategies, news, and personal experiences. You can participate in discussions, ask questions, and gather tips all from the comfort of your home. However, it's important to remember that not all advice found online is reliable. New traders, in particular, may struggle to distinguish between good advice and tips that could lead them astray. Always be sure to verify any information you come across.

Additionally, consider local meetups or trading clubs. Websites like Meetup.co m can help you find trading groups in your area. Connecting with other traders in person can help you build valuable relationships, and discussing strategies or trends face-to-face can significantly enhance your understanding of the market.

Sharing Experiences and Strategies

Once you've found a community that feels right for you, engage by sharing your own trading experiences and strategies. By putting yourself out there, you invite feedback, which can provide you with new perspectives on your trading. It's a mutual exchange: you gain insights from their suggestions, and they learn from what you share. This kind of collaboration benefits everyone involved.

If you're interested, consider starting a blog or vlog to document your trading journey. Share the strategies you're trying, what works, what doesn't, and all the ups and downs you encounter. Make it interactive by inviting comments and suggestions. This practice not only helps you reflect on your trading but may also assist others who are facing similar challenges.

Professional Networking Events

Professional trading events and conferences provide numerous opportunities to meet individuals who are passionate about trading. These gatherings attract traders and experts from all areas of finance. For instance, events like the Traders Expo offer workshops, seminars, and ample chances to connect with experienced traders and industry professionals.

When you attend these events, be proactive in engaging with others. Participate in discussions, exchange contact information, and follow up afterward. The relationships you build at these events could lead to collaborations, mentorships, or partnerships that may enhance your trading efforts.

Networking can be a significant game-changer. It opens doors to new learning opportunities, personal growth, and teamwork. By connecting with trading communities, sharing your experiences, and attending events, you set yourself up for a more fulfilling trading journey. Step out of your trading room, make those connections, and you might discover that it's one of the smartest moves you can make.

10.4 Keeping Up With Regulatory Changes in Options Trading

Regulatory agencies closely monitor financial markets, and their rules can significantly impact how you trade. In the U.S., organizations like the Securities and Exchange Commission (SEC) and the Commodity Futures Trading Commission (CFTC) play crucial roles in ensuring that the market remains fair and transparent. Their primary objective is to protect investors from fraud and to regulate trading practices.

Staying up-to-date with regulatory changes is not just about adhering to rules; it's also essential for protecting your investments and ensuring your trading strategies remain effective. A straightforward way to stay informed is by subscribing to newsletters from these regulatory bodies or reputable industry groups. These newsletters typically break down recent updates, explain how changes might affect traders, and provide tips for maintaining compliance.

Some updates, such as changes to margin requirements, can influence the capital available for trading, potentially altering your trading volume or strategy. Being proactive about these changes means understanding what has changed and adjusting your strategies accordingly. You may need to refine your trading approach, revisit your risk management plan, or explore new platforms or tools to ensure you're aligned with the latest rules.

If keeping track of these updates feels overwhelming, there are resources available to assist you. Compliance consultants specialize in helping traders understand and adhere to financial regulations. They can provide tailored advice to ensure you are trading within the rules. Legal advisors knowledgeable in securities law can also be beneficial, especially if new regulations affect your trading setup or tax obligations. Additionally, many trading platforms now offer tools that assist with compliance by tracking your trades, generating reports, and flagging potential issues, allowing you to concentrate on your trading.

10.5 Planning for Tax Implications of Trading Gains

Understanding the tax rules on trading gains is crucial for any trader. In the U.S., for instance, the distinction between short-term and long-term capital gains can significantly impact your tax obligations. Gains from assets held for less than a year are taxed as regular income, which can be as high as 37%. Conversely, gains from assets held for more than a year are taxed at lower rates, typically capping at 20%. This is why many traders pay close attention to the duration of their investments. It's not just about how much you earn; it's also about how much you keep after taxes.

Keeping Accurate Records

Just as keeping records can help you reflect on past decisions, maintaining accurate and detailed records of your trading activities is essential for tax purposes. This involves tracking all your trades as well as any related expenses, such as software subscriptions, home office costs, or educational materials. These records will be valuable not only when you file your taxes but also in the event of an audit. Using trade accounting software can simplify this process by automatically logging your trades, tracking your expenses, and storing everything in one convenient location.

Tax-Optimization Strategies

As you become more familiar with trading, you may want to explore methods for reducing your tax bill. One well-known strategy is tax-loss harvesting, which involves selling investments at a loss to offset capital gains. This approach can lower your taxable income and reduce the taxes you owe on your profits.

Another option is to utilize specific accounts, such as an IRA or a 401(k), for your trading activities. These accounts offer tax benefits; trades made within them can grow either tax-free or tax-deferred, which can significantly impact your overall financial plan.

Each strategy has its own details, so it's important to work with a tax professional and choose the one that aligns best with your financial goals and situation.

Consulting with Tax Professionals

Even with careful planning, tax laws can be complicated—especially if you trade frequently or engage in complex transactions. This is where tax professionals can help. Collaborating with a CPA or tax advisor who specializes in investment taxes can be a significant advantage. These experts provide personalized advice based on your specific situation, assist you in navigating deductions, and clarify intricate tax laws. Additionally, they can help you prepare for future tax scenarios based on your trading strategies, ensuring that you remain fully compliant. This allows you to focus more on trading and worry less about the tax implications.

10.6 Evaluating Trading Performance and Making Adjustments

As a trader, it's important to regularly assess your progress and make adjustments as necessary to stay on track. Reviewing your trades consistently allows you to maximize your profits, manage risks effectively, and learn from your past experiences.

Performance Metrics

To effectively assess your performance, it's important to understand some key metrics, such as profit and loss, return on investment (ROI), and risk/reward ratio. Profit and loss provide a basic overview of your overall gains or losses. ROI helps you evaluate how well your trades are performing in relation to the amount you invested. The risk/reward ratio illustrates the relationship between potential gains and the risks associated with each trade. Monitoring these metrics can guide your decisions on when to play it safe and when to take calculated risks.

Regular Review Cycles

Establishing regular times to review your trades is a beneficial practice. Some traders conduct these reviews weekly, while others prefer a monthly schedule. Choose a schedule that works best for you. During these reviews, look for patterns in your trading. Do some strategies yield consistent results, while others result in losses? Analyzing your trades more closely will help you identify what is effective and where improvements are needed.

Adapting Trading Strategies

Learning from these reviews can help you refine your strategies. The market is constantly changing, and a strategy that was effective last month may need some adjustments now. If you observe that a strategy tends to underperform during turbulent market conditions, consider adding protective measures or temporarily avoiding its use during volatile periods. Conversely, if a strategy is yielding strong results, you might explore safe ways to enhance it. Adjusting strategies doesn't require drastic changes; instead, it involves making thoughtful modifications based on current market trends.

Learning from Mistakes

Learning from mistakes is a significant aspect of achieving success in trading. When a trade doesn't go as planned, it's important to analyze what went wrong. Was it due to the strategy, a missed market signal, or something unexpected? Documenting these insights can help you avoid similar errors in the future. Additionally, sharing your experiences with other traders can provide new perspectives or advice you might not have considered.

Regularly reviewing your trading performance and making small, data-driven adjustments keep your strategies aligned with market changes and your personal goals. This proactive approach ensures that your trading continues to improve over time.

CONCLUSION

BEFORE WE WRAP UP, let's recap what we've covered. We started with the fundamentals of market analysis, discussed individual options instruments, and then combined these concepts to create bull puts and bear calls. Finally, we explored iron condors, all to provide you with a solid foundation and strategies that can enhance your trading in any market.

Don't underestimate the value of connecting with other traders. Trading doesn't have to be a solo endeavor. Having others to exchange ideas with and learn from can be a significant advantage.

Now, it's time to put these ideas into action. Start small, apply the strategies we discussed, and build a portfolio that aligns with your goals and risk tolerance. Remember, trading is more than just making money—it's about developing good habits for the long term.

Thank you for taking the time to engage with this book. Your presence here indicates your commitment to learning about options trading. Keep pushing forward, stay curious, and maintain connections with others who share your interest in trading. I would love to hear about your journey, including your successes and the lessons you learned along the way.

Let's continue exploring trading together. With focus, curiosity, and the tips you've acquired here, you're on the path to making options trading a meaningful part of your financial journey. Here's to your success!

References

Babson College. (n.d.). *Technical analysis: Getting started.* Retrieved from: https://www.babson.edu/media/babson/assets/cutler-center/Introduciton-to-Technical-Analysis.pdf

Business Fundas. (2024). *The importance of continuous learning in trading.* Retrieved from: https://www.business-fundas.com/2024/the-importance-of-continuous-learning-in-trading/

Chauhan, A. (n.d.). *Importance and benefits of paper trading.* Retrieved from: https://www.linkedin.com/pulse/importance-benefits-paper-trading-atul-chauhan-l6dtc

Corporate Finance Institute. (n.d.). *Market sentiment - Definition, indicator types, strategies.* Retrieved from: https://corporatefinanceinstitute.com/resources/career-map/sell-side/capital-markets/market-sentiment/

HighStrike. (n.d.). *6 tips for trading with a full-time job.* Retrieved from: https://highstrike.medium.com/6-tips-for-trading-with-a-full-time-job-c58333949f99

Investopedia. (n.d.). *12 things you need to know about financial statements.* Retrieved from: https://www.investopedia.com/articles/basics/06/financialreporting.asp

Investopedia. (2024). *Best options trading platforms of 2024.* Retrieved from: https://www.investopedia.com/best-brokers-for-options-trading-4587876

Investopedia. (n.d.). *Gamma hedging: Definition, how it works, and vs. delta.* Retrieved from: https://www.investopedia.com/terms/g/gamma-hedging.asp

Investopedia. (n.d.). *Implied volatility: Buy low and sell high.* Retrieved from: https://www.investopedia.com/articles/optioninvestor/08/implied-volatility.asp

Investopedia. (n.d.). *Options basics: How to pick the right strike price.* Retrieved from: https://www.investopedia.com/articles/active-trading/021014/options-basics-how-pick-right-strike-price.asp

Investopedia. (n.d.). *Options trading with the iron condor.* Retrieved from: https://www.investopedia.com/articles/optioninvestor/06/ironcondor.asp

Investopedia. (n.d.). *The stop-loss order—Make sure you use it.* Retrieved from: https://www.investopedia.com/articles/stocks/09/use-stop-loss.asp

Investopedia. (n.d.). *Top 7 books to learn technical analysis for stocks.* Retrieved from: https://www.investopedia.com/articles/personal-finance/090916/top-5-books-learn-technical-analysis.asp

Investopedia. (n.d.). *Using the "Greeks" to understand options.* Retrieved from: https://www.investopedia.com/trading/using-the-greeks-to-understand-options/

Investopedia. (n.d.). *Best options trading platforms of 2024.* Retrieved from: https://www.investopedia.com/best-brokers-for-options-trading-4587876

Moneywise. (2023). *The best options trading platforms 2023.* Retrieved from: https://moneywise.com/investing/stocks/best-options-trading-platforms

NerdWallet. (n.d.). *Options trading: Step-by-step guide for beginners.* Retrieved from:
https://www.nerdwallet.com/article/investing/how-to-trade-options

Option Alpha. (n.d.). *Building a diversified options portfolio.* Retrieved from: https://optionalpha.com/lessons/building-diversified-options-portfolio

Option Alpha. (n.d.). *How to adjust a losing credit spread option strategy.* Retrieved from:
https://optionalpha.com/blog/how-to-adjust-a-losing-credit-spread

Option Samurai. (n.d.). *Credit spread option strategy.* Retrieved from: https://blog.optionsamurai.com/credit-spread-option-strategy/

ORATS. (2024). *Best options backtesting platforms in 2024.* Retrieved from: https://orats.com/blog/best-options-backtesting-platforms-in-2024

Samco. (n.d.). *How to use options trading calculators to plan your trades.* Retrieved from:
https://www.samco.in/knowledge-center/articles/options-trading-calculators/

Schwab. (n.d.). *Reducing risk with a credit spread options strategy.* Retrieved from:
https://www.schwab.com/learn/story/reducing-risk-with-credit-spread-options-strategy

Schwab. (n.d.). *The risks of options assignment.* Retrieved from: https://www.schwab.com/learn/story/risks-options-assignment

Schwab. (n.d.). *Three options trading adjustment strategies.* Retrieved from: https://www.schwab.com/learn/story/three-options-trading-adjustment-strategies

SMB Training. (n.d.). *The value of building a trading/investing network.* Retrieved from: https://www.smbtraining.com/blog/the-value-of-building-a-tradinginvesting-network

TastyLive. (n.d.). *High implied volatility strategies.* Retrieved from: https://www.tastylive.com/definitions/high-implied-volatility-strategies

TastyLive. (n.d.). *Implied volatility (IV) in options trading explained.* Retrieved from: https://www.tastylive.com/concepts-strategies/implied-volatility

The Motley Fool. (n.d.). *Call vs. put options: What's the difference?* Retrieved from: https://www.fool.com/investing/how-to-invest/stocks/call-options-vs-put-options/

U.S. Internal Revenue Service. (n.d.). *Topic no. 429, traders in securities (information for form ...).*
Retrieved from: https://www.irs.gov/taxtopics/tc429

www.ingramcontent.com/pod-product-compliance
Lightning Source LLC
LaVergne TN
LVHW052026200926
848481LV00005B/1598
* 9 7 9 8 3 4 8 4 6 9 6 9 6 *